The Vacuum
of Unbelief

The Vacuum
of Unbelief

AND OTHER ESSAYS

by
STUART BARTON BABBAGE

ZONDERVAN PUBLISHING HOUSE
GRAND RAPIDS, MICHIGAN

FOREWORD

There is a real need today for the presentation of Christian truth in forms which can be readily understood and appreciated. The ordinary man is not inclined to endure the discipline of reading long and erudite works on theology. Still less is he likely to read a collection of sermons, excellent though these may be in content and in form.

In this volume the author has set himself the task of presenting a variety of Christian themes in the form of essays which in themselves make easy and pleasant reading. Each chapter of the book is complete in itself and can be read with profit apart from its companions. At the same time, there is a basic unity of purpose running through the volume which provides cumulative effect and makes it inviting and rewarding as a whole.

Christian thought and action have too often been presented in a way which makes them seem unrelated to other aspects of the world in which modern man finds himself. In these chapters, however, one finds profound truths of the Christian faith illumined by countless references to and quotations from a variety of authors, mostly secular. The ideas which they embody are skillfully set in the context of the twentieth century and related to events and problems which are familiar to us all. One can scarcely read the book without obtaining new insights into the nature of the world in which we live or without finding stimulus to further study of literature and of history.

Dr. Babbage has been well-prepared for his writing by encyclopedic reading and by a distinguished career as churchman and educator both in Australia and in the United States of America. During recent years he has served as Professor of Practical Apologetics at Columbia Theological Seminary, Decatur, Georgia. As a man deeply committed to the historic Christian faith, he has sought in teaching, as he does in this book, to set forth the enduring relationship between Christianity and Culture — between the Christian and the society in which he lives.

The non-technical nature of these essays is designed to make them valuable to the layman as well as to the scholar. They should have a strong appeal for young people as well as for those who are older. Intensely practical in nature, they will also serve as an invitation to scholarship and to clear thinking. For these reasons it is a pleasure to commend them to the careful attention of the reader, and to wish for them a wide circulation.

J. McDowell Richards
President,
Columbia Theological Seminary

CONTENTS

Foreword

PART I

PART II

PART I

Chapter One

THE VACUUM OF UNBELIEF

Hanging in the library of Fitzwilliam Hall, Cambridge, England, are two characteristic cartoons by Sir Max Beerbohm. The first depicts a tall corpulent man, who, with proud and approving self-complacency, is gazing in a mirror at a larger reflection of himself. The second depicts a diminutive man, who, dressed immaculately in evening clothes, is wearing a black crepe armband. He is gazing apprehensively at the horizon, over which there hangs a giant question mark like a baleful star. The first cartoon symbolizes the smug self-satisfaction of the nineteenth century; the second, the anxious perplexity of the twentieth.

Unhappily, the question mark today bears the ominous shape of a mushroom cloud. In this twentieth century, despite the spectacular achievements of a technological civilization, we all live in secret fear of nuclear annihilation.

Omar Bradley, in a neat epigram, says that we are "nuclear giants and moral babes." [1] By a hideous irony, we are in imminent danger of being destroyed by the Frankenstein monster we ourselves have created.

Where is guidance to be found? Is there an answer to our human dilemma?

I

Ought we to look to the university to provide us with saving advice? The problem, Sir Walter Moberly notes, in

[1] Quoted, Leighton Ford, *The Christian Persuader* (New York: Harper & Row, 1966), p. 26. Quoted by permission.

his important study *The Crisis in the University,* is that today the university lives and moves and has its being in a
moral and cultural fog. He writes:

> If you want a bomb the chemists' department will teach
> you how to make it; if you want a cathedral the depart-
> ment of architecture will teach you how to build it; if you
> want a healthy body the department of physiology and
> medicine will teach you how to tend it. But when you
> ask whether and why you should want bombs or cathe-
> drals or healthy bodies, the university is dumb and silent.
> It can help and give guidance in all things subsidiary but
> not in the attainment of the one thing needful.[2]

The fact is that we all too often confine education to the
use of means as opposed to the choice of ends, to training in
the handling and acquisition of tools to the neglect of the
purposes for which those tools are to be used. If students
cannot get guidance for action from their teachers they will
seek it, he warns, from less reputable sources. It was thus
that, thirty years ago, the students of Germany fell victims
to Hitler. As Professor R. G. Collingwood reminds us, they
will infer that for guidance in the problems of life, since they
cannot get it from thinkers or from thinking, from ideals or
from principles, they must look to people who are not
thinkers, but fools; to processes that are not thinking, but
passion; to aims that are not ideals but caprices; and to rules
that are not principles, but expediency. [3]

II

Our Lord Jesus Christ told a grim and creepy story about
an empty house and an undesirable tenant. A house, Jesus
related, fell into evil hands. The owner turned the undesirable tenant out and did the place up from floor to ceiling.
Then he left it, clean, but unoccupied. One day the old
tenant passed it again. He had found no suitable alternative
home. He saw the house was empty. He went and peered

[2] (London: S.C.M. Press, 1949). p. 52. Quoted by permission.
[3] Quoted, *Ibid,* p. 54.

in at the windows and tried the doors. Then calling to him a group of still more undesirable friends he forced his way in and took possession. And soon the house was in a worse state than ever (Luke 11:24-26).

That house, Jesus explained, was a human personality. The undesirable tenant was an evil spirit which a man had cast out of his life. The spirit came back from wandering restlessly about the desert and found an empty soul. The man had invited no good angels to tenant his life. So the evil spirit found seven other devils more evil than himself. ". . . and they enter and dwell there; and the last state of that man becomes worse than the first."

III

No one can deny that, in this twentieth century, the universities have been responsible for casting out the devils of ignorance and superstition, the devils of darkness and error, but what has taken their place? Has the house been left clean and empty? Is there, in the minds of students which have been swept and clean, a moral and spiritual vacuum?

We have lived to see, in this country, the betrayal of the universities. How do we explain the disconcerting fact, Sir Walter Moberly pointedly asks, that the universities of Germany, in the days of Hitler, capitulated to doctrines that were morally monstrous and intellectually despicable? How do we explain the fact that places dedicated to the pursuit of liberty and freedom surrendered to doctrines of racial superiority and Nordic purity? The German universities, in the days before Hitler, enjoyed an intellectual prestige second to none. How do we explain the measure of their betrayal? Was it due to the fact that the German universities had no independent standards of value of which they felt themselves to be the guardians? Was this the reason that they lacked sufficient conviction and tenacity of purpose to stand against the torrential tide of Nazi tyranny?

Whatever the explanation, it is an incontrovertible fact

that, in the day of trial and testing, it was the Church that stood alone. Albert Einstein [4] publicly testified:

> I looked to the universities to defend freedom, but the universities were silenced in a few short weeks . . . Only the Church stood squarely across the path of Hitler's campaign for the suppression of truth . . . I am forced to confess that what I once despised I now praise.

IV

We are, in America, rightly concerned with driving out and banishing from the lives of men the devils of prejudice and passion, of ignorance and darkness, of superstition and error. Have good angels been invited in to take possession? Or is the house swept — and empty?

There are, unhappily, other devils, more deadly than the first, waiting to take possession.

Marxist Communism is ready to take possession. It is ready to take possession because there is a spiritual emptiness in the lives of many students today. "It will be hard indeed," Arnold Toynbee sadly comments, "to refill the spiritual vacuum which is being hollowed in our western hearts by the progressive decay of religious belief." [5]

The experience of Freda Utley illustrates the nature of our predicament. She was a brilliant American student who married a Russian expatriate Jew. Together they resolved that they would return to Russia to serve the Soviet Fatherland. Her husband disappeared during the paranoic purges of Stalin in 1937. She tells us in her book, *Lost Illusion*,[6] what moved her to embrace Communism. It was, she confides, the consciousness of a spiritual vacuum. She was secretly looking for a faith to believe and a flag to follow and a song

[4] Albert Einstein was a German-born physicist; he became an American citizen in 1940; he introduced the theory of relativity, and received the Nobel prize in physics in 1921.

[5] Toynbee has expounded this theme in several places. See, *An Historian's Approach to Religion* (New York: Oxford University Press, 1956), pp. 180, 182, 208, 212, 213, 214, 226; *Civilization on Trial* (New York: Oxford University Press, 1948), p. 208.

[6] (Chicago: Henry Regnery, 1948).

to sing. The instinctive desire for religion, was the compelling force which led her, step by step, into the communist trap.

Douglas Hyde's experience was not dissimilar. He was, for many years, Secretary of the Communist Party in Great Britain. In his autobiography, *I Believed*, he explains that Communism was, for him, a substitute religion. It filled the gap. "Communism," he explains, "has had its origins in precisely that spiritual vacuum which exists all over what once was Christendom." "One has to be potentially good or intelligent," he insists, "even to be aware that it is not enough simply to drift along without sense of purpose or direction, with neither faith nor ideal. That is why Communism so often claims the best — those who feel the miss. It is why it has spread in our day and no other." "I would say," he accuses, "that the majority who come to Communism do so because, in the first instance, they are subconsciously looking for a cause which will fill the void left by unbelief." [7]

R. H. Crossman, who is now a member of Harold Wilson's Labor Cabinet, wrote, some years ago, an introduction to a symposium entitled, *The God That Failed*. In this book the contributors relate the factors that led them to embrace Communism, and the events which led to a subsequent repudiation. Arthur Koestler bitterly testifies:

> I served the Communist Party for seven years — the same length of time Jacob tended Laban's sheep to win Rachel his daughter. When the time was up, the bride was led into his dark tent; only the next morning did he discover that his ardors had been spent not on the lovely Rachel but on the ugly Leah.
>
> I wonder whether he ever recovered from the shock of having slept with an illusion. I wonder whether afterwards he believed that he had ever believed in it. [8]

Every revolution, Dean Inge avers, begins by proclaiming that we have nothing to lose but our chains and ends by

[7] (London: William Heinemann, 1952), p. 273. Quoted by permission.
[8] (New York: Harper, 1950), p. 82. Quoted by permission.

binding our feet in fresh fetters of iron. [9] Communism is no exception. It proclaims that man is born free and that everywhere he is in chains; it ends by enslaving men in the bitter bondage of *Animal Farm.* It promises, Inge repeats, "an earthly paradise at the end of a flowery path, and gives us a premature hell at the end of a way of blood." [10]

Communists know our moral vulnerability. They know there is a vacuum left by modern unbelief. They know that the heart of Western man is swept — and empty. And they are ready and eager to take possession.

V

But there are other devils who are ready to take possession.

Scientific Rationalism is always ready. The recent flight of the American astronauts is simply a further stage in a spectacular series of steadily mounting achievements. It is not surprising that, for many, science is a god opening the door to a vista of limitless advance. Lewis Mumford concludes his monumental study *Technics and Civilization* with the confident assertion: "Nothing is impossible." [11] Sir Richard Gregory, the editor of the scientific journal *Nature* says:

> My grandfather preached the gospel of Christ,
> My father preached the gospel of Socialism,
> I preach the gospel of Science. [12]

It is at the altar of science that multitudes today idolatrously worship. And the reason is not hard to find. We have all benefited from the solid and substantial achievements of science, and, in our simple naivety, we are tempted to believe that there are no problems which science cannot solve.

[9] W. R. Inge, *The Fall of the Idols* (London: Putnam, 1940), p. 84. Quoted by permission.
[10] W. R. Inge, *Talks in a Free Country* (London: Putnam, 1942), p. 27. Quoted by permission.
[11] (New York: Harcourt Brace & Co. 1934), p. 435.
[12] Quoted, C. A. Coulson, *Science and Christian Belief* (Chapel Hill: U.N.C. Press, 1955), p. 7. Quoted by permission.

There are some, however, who fear that science may equally well be our destroyer. Pierre Curie, the discoverer of radium, had serious doubts about man's moral maturity. "One may imagine," he warns, "that in criminal hands radium might become very dangerous, and that we may ask ourselves if humanity has anything to gain by learning the secrets of nature, if it is ripe enough to profit by them, or if this knowledge is not harmful." [13]

H. G. Wells is, perhaps, typical. In his younger days he was enthusiastic about *The Shape of Things to Come* (to appropriate the title of one of his best known tales of science fiction). With the outbreak of war, he saw, with incredulity and despair, the dedication of science to purposes of diabolical destruction. Shortly before his death he bitterly confessed:

> But quite apart from any bodily depression, the spectacle of evil in the world — the wanton destruction of homes, the ruthless hounding of decent folk into exile, the bombings of open cities, the cold-blooded massacres and mutilations of children and defenseless gentle folk, the rapes and filthy humiliations and, above all, the return of deliberate and organized torture, mental torment and fear to a world from which such things had seemed well nigh banished — has come near to breaking my spirit altogether. [14]

After the atomic destruction of Hiroshima, J. R. Oppenheimer, the American atomic physicist, pointed out that scientists are not exempt from human culpability and guilt: "In some crude sense, which no vulgarity, no humor, no overstatement can quite extinguish, the physicists have known sin; and this is a knowledge which they cannot lose." [15]

Aldous Huxley was acutely aware of the potential dangers that threaten the world through the perverted use of science.

[13] Quoted, *The Era of Atomic Power: Report of a Commission appointed by the British Council of Churches* (London: S.C.M. Press, 1946), p. 65.
[14] *The Fate of Man* (New York: Longmans, Green & Co., 1939), pp. 106-7. Quoted by permission.
[15] Quoted, C. A. Coulson, *Science, Technology and the Christian* (Tennessee: Abingdon, 1960), p. 120. Quoted by permission.

In his mordant satire, *Brave New World*, he is concerned to demonstrate what may happen if the conditioners of the human personality have their way. Through the awful instrumentality of a perverted science we may find, he urgently warns, that we have accomplished our own dehumanization.

VI

How, then, are we to avoid the specious seduction of Marxism on the one hand and the no less sinister seduction of Scientific Rationalism on the other? How are we to safeguard the citadels of our personality from sabotage and attack?

The house, in the parable, was swept and empty. But no good tenant had taken possession. "The devils," Dag Hammarskjold notes, "enter uninvited when the house stands empty. For other kinds of guests, you have first to open the door." [16]

The question, then, is whether we are going to allow the rightful owner to come in and take possession, or whether we are going to allow, by indolence or ignorance, Satanic forces to seduce us and subdue us? "Behold," Jesus says, "I stand at the door and knock; if any one hears my voice and opens the door, I will come in to him and eat with him, and he with me" (Revelation 3:20).

If the Lord Jesus occupies the citadel of our hearts, the evil spirits of this present age may peer in at the window, they may rattle at the doors, but they will not find an entrance.

[16] *Markings* (New York: Alfred A. Knopf, 1964), p. 12. Quoted by permission.

Chapter Two

RABBITS' PAWS

We are, Clement Rogers reminds us,[1] surrounded by superstition: superstition about doing things on Friday; about
touching wood for luck; about passing under a ladder (even
when there is no danger of having paint splashed on you);
superstition about unlucky numbers (I have, for example,
at different times, lived, both in England and in Australia,
in a house which was numbered 11a, instead of 13, so that
the series ran 7, 9, 11, 11a, 15, 17); superstition about up-
setting salt; about charms and mascots; about picking up
pins; about lucky horseshoes and rabbits' paws.

There are also happenings taken as bad omens: an ordinary hearse, for example, meeting a wedding procession; a
picture falling from the wall; a new moon seen through
glass (which is very hard on those of us who have the mis-
fortune to wear eye glasses); and breaking a looking glass.

People must believe something. If they have nothing
sensible to believe, then they will believe nonsense. It is a
fact commonly observed that when faith in God decays,
superstition grows; and today, with the withering of faith,
we see the flowering of credulity.

I

During the war years the use of charms and mascots
greatly increased, and Geoffrey Gorer, in an important
study, *Exploring English Character,* says that those who

---

[1] *Astrology and Prediction* (London: S.C.M. Press, 1948).

carry a lucky charm number no less than fifteen per cent of the population. During World War II one person in three had his or her private piece of solid magic: the scarf of a favorite girl, a lucky penny, a Cupid or a Mickey Mouse. Even crosses, Prayer Books and Testaments were frequently carried, not for reasons of piety, but for protection.

Geoffrey Gorer discovered that four-fifths of the population reads a horoscope every week, although the lower the income the higher the readership, and the higher the age the higher the readership! No less than half the population, he informs us, has consulted a fortune teller at some time or other.

Shortly after World War II a newspaper report was published concerning an enterprising Australian businessman who was preparing for export half a million rabbits' paws for use as pendants and as catches on ladies' purses. The front paws, he reported, are particularly lucky. (Hemingway, in his younger days, according to his own testimony in *A Movable Feast*, always carried around a nearly worn-out rabbit's foot.)

All this means that a quarter of the population has adopted a view of the universe which can most properly be designated as magical. Multitudes believe that the future is arbitrarily pre-determined; they believe that it is knowable by certain techniques; they believe that evil can be averted by the employment of mascots and the use of certain devices, and that good can be secured by the same simple and convenient means. It is important to notice that there is no connection between effort and reward, transgression and punishment.

Christians do not subscribe to this view: they believe that, behind the universe, there is One whose purposes are purposes of love, whose works are right and whose ways are just (Daniel 4:37).

II

Historically, superstition has taken four main forms: astrology, magic, witchcraft, and spiritualism.

Astrology is the belief that a man's destiny is determined
by his horoscope: that is, by the plan and pattern of the sky
in relation to the signs of the zodiac at the time of his birth.

The Babylonians, who made the stars a subject of intense
observation, noticed that some stars remain in their places,
rising and setting, but that others, and those among the
highest, move irregularly. These stars (named "planets")
were, they believed, the homes of gods who powerfully in-
fluence the lives of men. From Babylonia these beliefs
entered the Graeco-Roman world. "On even the slightest
motion of the stars hang the fortunes of nations," Seneca
writes, "and the greatest and smallest events are shaped
to accord with the progress of a kindly or unkindly star."

There were many, however, who treated these doctrines
with satiric scepticism. Plato ridicules the cult of astrology;
Aristotle scorns it; Cicero condemns it. The Jews held that
the planets were not the homes of gods or of demons but the
handiwork of God (Psalm 19:1). Isaiah speaks of astrol-
ogers with contemptuous scorn: "Let them stand forth
and save you, those who divide the heavens, who gaze at
the stars, who at the new moons predict what shall befall
you" (Isaiah 47:13).

Today, the educated man knows that the science of astrology is a fraud and a fiction. We no longer ask incredulously:

> Twinkle, twinkle, little star,
> How I wonder what you are!

We know the answer:

> You're the cooling down of gases
> Into incandescent masses.

Nevertheless, in spite of the fact that we know these
things, we are still intrigued and impressed by the prognos-
tications of the horoscope. We hear what we want to hear:
that we are neither responsible for our faults nor answerable
for our failures. Cassius knew better:

> "The fault, dear Brutus, is not in our stars,
> But in ourselves, that we are underlings."

III

Secondly, there is magic. Magic is the belief that certain things and particular objects possess hidden powers. Magic is a relic of primitive paganism and the cult of animism: it is the belief that there are spirits who reside in stones and springs, plants and animals, and that by certain manipulative devices we can share their power. This ancient belief finds contemporary expression in the faithful wearing of mascots and the use of talismans.

IV

Thirdly, there is witchcraft. Witchcraft credits certain people with special powers, powers which are believed to come from compacts with evil spirits.

The scapegoat in the Old Testament was the creature on which the sins of the people were laid before it was sent into the wilderness to die. Society tends to make scapegoats of those it fears. Once it was the physically deformed and the mentally deranged; today, it is the Jew and the Negro. Once it was sufficient to allege a secret alliance with the devil to secure a condemnation; today, it is sufficient, as Senator McCarthy discovered, to allege a secret affiliation with the Communist Party.

Arthur Miller's play, *The Crucible,* whose ostensible theme is the notorious witch trials at Salem, illustrates the manner in which prejudice and suspicion may be used by unscrupulous parties to create fear and terror in a community.

Years later, those who had served as jurors at Salem, issued a courageous retractation of their errors:

> We do therefore hereby signify to all in general (and to the surviving sufferers in special) our deep sense of, and sorrow for, our errors, in acting on such evidence to the condemning of any person; and do hereby declare, that we justly fear that we were sadly deluded and mistaken; for which we are much disquieted and distressed in our minds; and do therefore humbly beg forgiveness, first of God for Christ's sake, for this our error; and pray that God would not impute the guilt of it to ourselves, nor others; and we

also pray that we may be considered candidly, and aright, by the living sufferers, as being then under the power of a strong and general delusion, utterly unacquainted with, and not experienced in, matters of that nature.

We do heartily ask forgiveness of you all whom we have justly offended; and do declare, according to our present minds, we would none of us do such things again on such grounds for the whole world; praying you to accept of this in way of satisfaction for our offense, and that you would bless the inheritance of the Lord, that he may be entreated for the land. [2]

Hegel cynically comments: "What experience and history teach is this — that people and governments have never learned anything from history." Despite the somber lessons of the past, we have lived to see, in this twentieth century, the calculated cultivation of hysteria in the service of the omnicompetent state and the systematic extermination of six million Jews.

V

Fourthly, there is spiritualism. Spiritualism is the belief that communications are possible with the dead, who are assumed to have knowledge about the future.

The most powerful illustration in literature of a seance is the account of Saul's dramatic visit to the Witch of Endor:

Then Saul said to his servants, "Seek out for me a woman who is a medium, that I may go to her and inquire of her." And his servants said to him, "Behold, there is a medium at Endor."

So Saul disguised himself and put on other garments, and went, he and two men with him; and they came to the woman by night. And he said, "Divine for me by a spirit, and bring up for me whomever I shall name to you." The woman said to him, "Surely you know what Saul has done, how he has cut off the mediums and the wizards from the land. Why then are you laying a snare for my life to bring about my death?" But Saul swore to her by the Lord, "As

[2] Quoted, Charles Williams, *Witchcraft* (New York: Meridian Books, 1959), p. 293.

the Lord lives, no punishment shall come upon you for this thing." Then the woman said, "Whom shall I bring up for you?" He said, "Bring up Samuel for me."

When the woman saw Samuel, she cried out with a loud voice; and the woman said to Saul, "Why have you deceived me? You are Saul." The king said to her, "Have no fear; what do you see?" And the woman said to Saul, "I see a god coming up out of the earth." He said to her, "What is his appearance?" And she said, "An old man is coming up; and he is wrapped in a robe." And Saul knew that it was Samuel, and he bowed with his face to the ground, and did obeisance.

Then Samuel said to Saul, "Why have you disturbed me by bringing me up?" Saul answered, "I am in great distress; for the Philistines are warring against me, and God has turned away from me and answers me no more, either by prophets or by dreams; therefore I have summoned you to tell me what I shall do." And Samuel said, "Why then do you ask me, since the Lord has turned from you and become your enemy? The Lord has done to you as he spoke by me; for the Lord has torn the kingdom out of your hand, and given it to your neighbor, David. Because you did not obey the voice of the Lord, and did not carry out his fierce wrath against Amalek, therefore the Lord has done this thing to you this day. Moreover the Lord will give Israel also with you into the hand of the Philistines; and tomorrow you and your sons shall be with me; the Lord will give the army of Israel also into the hand of the Philistines."

Then Saul fell at once full length upon the ground, filled with fear because of the words of Samuel; and there was no strength in him, for he had eaten nothing all day and all night. And the woman came to Saul, and when she saw that he was terrified, she said to him, "Behold, your handmaid has hearkened to you; I have taken my life in my hand, and have hearkened to what you have said to me. Now therefore, you also hearken to your handmaid; let me set a morsel of bread before you; and eat, that you may have strength when you go on your way." He refused, and said, "I will not eat." But his servants, together with the woman, urged him; and he hearkened to their words. So he arose from the earth, and sat upon the bed. Now the woman had a fatted calf in the house, and she quickly killed it, and she took flour, and kneaded it and baked unleavened bread of it, and she put it before Saul and his servants; and they ate. Then they rose and went away that night (I Samuel 28:7-25).

In our day, with its erosion of faith, men have become increasingly skeptical about life beyond the grave. It is not surprising that some are tempted to seek the services of those who assert that they are able to communicate with the dead. What is depressing is the nature and quality of the communications purported to be received. Dean Inge observes that "the kind of survival which Sir Oliver Lodge and his disciples comfort themselves with imagining would add a new terror to death." [3] Concerning the so-called proofs of survival, T. H. Huxley says:

> The only good I can see in the demonstration of the truth of spiritualism is to furnish an additional argument against suicide. Better live a crossing sweeper than die and be made to talk twaddle by a 'medium' hired at a guinea a *seance.*

Christianity, of course, is not interested in the question of mere survival; what matters is the quality of life beyond the grave. What the creeds affirm is a life which is rich and full, splendid and transcendent: the resurrection of the body and life everlasting.

VI

Every form of superstition is an attempt to penetrate the unknown — either to forestall evil or to foretell the future. Men have always wanted to know. That is why, down the ages, they have consulted oracles and listened to the predictions of prophets and augurs, wizards and witches; that is why they have looked for omens in the flights of birds; that is why they have sacrificed animals and examined their entrails, interpreted dreams and believed in numbers, cast horoscopes and consulted the stars.

The "science" of prediction, however, is a fraud and a

[3] W. R. Inge, *Talks in a Free Country* (London: Putnam, 1942), p. 31.

snare; its professors are charlatans and rogues, and its followers dupes and fools.

Superstition is a substitute faith. It capitalizes and grows on ignorance and fear; it bewitches and bemuses the credulous and the gullible. It makes no moral nor ethical demands; it is selfish and self-centered; it is irrational and absurd.

Little, however, is achieved by exposing folly, and men are not converted by ridicule. The most powerful corrective of superstition is a right belief in God. " . . . religion," says Edmund Burke, "and not atheism, is the true remedy for superstition." [4] The answer to superstition is not no faith but right faith; not no belief but true belief. Thomas Chambers speaks of "the expulsive power of a new and a nobler affection." The best way to banish the darkness is to turn on the light; the best way to banish the darkness of superstition is to live in the light of God. In the film *Martin Luther,* Staupitz says: "If you take away the amulets and the beads . . . the rosary and the crucifix, what will you put in their place?" To which Luther makes the magnificent reply, "Christ!" That is all, but that is enough.

The prophet Isaiah indicates the nature of the alternative: "And when they say to you, 'Consult the mediums and the wizards who chirp and mutter,' should not a people consult their God? Should they consult the dead on behalf of the living?" (Isaiah 8:19).

"Superstition," Edmund Burke says tersely, "is the religion of feeble minds." [5] That is why the wise man will heed the advice of the prophet Isaiah: he will forswear and forsake rabbits' paws to seek and to serve the living God.

---

[4] *Speech on Conciliation with America,* 22 March, 1775.
[5] *Reflections on the Revolution in France*

Chapter Three

SEEKING A REWARD

An article on the attitudes and values of American students by a visiting exchange lecturer from England serving in the United States recently appeared in the pages of *The Twentieth Century*. The article was entitled, "Sex, Success and Sympathy." [1] American students, the writer asserts, are desperately anxious to abide by the values of their social group, to do the right thing, to conform to social patterns, and to achieve success. Most of them, he continues, think religion is a good thing: several students express the view that religion, among other things, gives you poise. It facilitates the process of psychological adjustment, it helps you to become a well-rounded personality. But religion does something else: it helps you to achieve social acceptance. "Religious qualities and high moral character," a freshman solemnly explains, "are essential to success." In the competitive struggle today, "the warmth derived from spiritual satisfaction is," we are informed, "a prime requisite to success." "Religion and business," another student points out, "serve one another."

I

Judging by these comments, the criteria by which religion ought to be judged is its utility. A student, commenting on how important it is to feel contented, and the business value of plentiful smiling, says: "In one of Dale Carnegie's books,

[1] "Sex, Success and Sympathy," by Malcolm Bradbury in *The Twentieth Century*, Vol. 161, No. 960, Feb., 1957.

he gives you six ways to make people like you. One thing he stresses is a ready smile. It not only makes you feel better, it helps your appearance."

Now the relevant question is this: Is religion in the same category as a course in the psychology of Dale Carnegie? Is the profession of religion a matter of careful calculation, a question of expediency, something that pays? Is religion, in essence, a technique for self-improvement, an easy and convenient road to success?

Jesus, in the days of His ministry, rebuked the insincerity of those Jews who sought Him, not because He was the truth, but because He gave them bread to eat. He knew, only too well, the empty significance of their patronage: ". . . you seek me," He bluntly told them, "not because you saw signs, but because you ate your fill of the loaves" (John 6:26). That was the plain and unpalatable truth: their enthusiasm was not disinterested — they sought Him because He had given them bread to eat. In like manner, there are those today who are ready to make a profession of religion for the solid and substantial benefits they hope to enjoy and the advantages they hope to gain. And what they forget is that God cannot be exploited, He can only be worshiped.

II

Let us speak in terms of greater particularity. The followers of Moral Re-Armament urgently declare that Christianity must be proclaimed in Africa and Asia: it is, they insist, the only possible defense against Communist infiltration and subversion. "We need," Frank N. D. Buchman proclaims, "to find an ideology that is big enough and complete enough to outmarch any of the other great ideologies." "Today we see three great ideologies battling for control. There is Fascism, and Communism, and there is that great other ideology which is the center of Christian Democracy — Moral Re-Armament." [2]

But we dare not use Christianity as a weapon with which

[2] Quoted, Peter Howard, *The World Rebuilt* (New York: Duell, Sloan & Pearce Press, 1951), pp. 126, 127. Quoted by permission.

to fight our political battles: the question is not whether
God is on the side of Western Democracy, but whether
Western Democracy is on the side of God. The Christian
faith ought to be proclaimed in Africa and Asia, not for
political reasons, as a bastion against Communism, but because it is the Gospel of God. We ought to proclaim Christianity, not for its consequences, but for itself; not because
it pays, but because it is true.

But we are also guilty here at home. From time to time
we seek to persuade men to attend church by the offer of
enticing inducements: even, it is alleged, by the offer of
Gold Bond stamps! A recent case achieved deserved notori-
ety. A local church, eager to improve the occasion, displayed
the crude and tasteless sign: "Come to church, and cure
your stomach ulcer!" What we have, of course, is the right
thing urged for the wrong reason. It is true that the person
who goes to church is less likely to suffer from stomach
ulcer than the person who consistently absents himself; it is
true that there is a therapeutic value in the confession of sin
and the gift of absolution and forgiveness; it is true that
those who worship God have a feeling of tranquillity, a sense
of inner peace. But these things are a by-product and not
an end, a gift and not a reward. The service of God, rightly
understood, is not a tranquilizing pill, nor is the worship of
God a sedative for tired and jaded spirits. The worship of
God is not an insurance policy against the slings and arrows
of outrageous fortune, as though the profession of the Christian faith exempted a man from the toils and tribulations
which are a part of our common lot. No! It is not for these
reasons that the Christian man serves God: he serves God,
not for His benefits, but for Himself.

There are some who are eager to prove the relevance of
religion in relation to the achievement of the good life. As
W. E. Sangster points out, "there are some realms where all
talk of 'relevance' is irrelevance. It introduces a test too
coarse to apply. It comes near to smearing the sanctities.
It demands to see the 'use' of things which soar above utilitarian tests and are right in themselves and not simply be-

cause of ends they serve." "For people who do believe in God," he rightly stresses, "evangelism is a duty and privilege so plain, so incontrovertible, that all talk of 'relevance' is a half-vulgar intrusion of the utilitarian into a realm where it cannot apply." [3]

Jesus, for His part, refused to win men by the offer of material rewards. In the wilderness He refused to turn stones into bread; He refused to win men by the offer of economic security. Jesus knew that man cannot live without bread, but He also knew that man cannot live by bread alone. After the feeding of the five thousand, Jesus was confronted by a renewal of the wilderness temptation. The crowd tried to take Him by force to make Him a king. Jesus immediately withdrew Himself from them. He knew the selfish motives which moved them, the material considerations which swayed them. He refused to be a party to their game.

When Jesus hung upon the cross He was vehemently urged to demonstrate the truth of His claims by exercising His divine power. "If you are the King of the Jews," they shouted, "save yourself!" (Luke 23:37). They tempted Him to use His divine power to compel belief, to win men by a spectacular demonstration of miraculous power. Jesus rejected the satanic invitation: He would win men by nothing save a cross, and He would offer to men nothing but a cross. "If any man would come after me," He said, "let him deny himself and take up his cross and follow me" (Matthew 16:24).

This is the theme of Dostoievsky's powerful prose poem, *The Grand Inquisitor.*

> Thou didst not come down from the Cross when they shouted to Thee, mocking and reviling Thee, "Come down from the cross and we will believe that Thou art He." Thou didst not come down, for again Thou wouldst not enslave men by a miracle, and didst crave faith given freely, not based on miracle. Thou didst crave for free love and not

[3] *Let me Commend* (Tennessee: Abingdon-Cokesbury, 1948), p. 12. Quoted by permission.

the base raptures of the slave before the might that has overawed him for ever. [4]

III

How are we seeking to win men? Are we degrading the service of God by pandering to man's deep cupidity? Are we preoccupied with the offer of tangible and material rewards? Are we unwittingly relegating the Sovereign Lord of the Universe, the Creator of heaven and earth, to the role of a magic charm or a lucky mascot?

There is only one adequate motive for worship and that is love, and there is only one adequate basis for service and that is gratitude. "The debt of love is permanent, for we must pay it daily, and yet always owe it," Origen says.

In the Nuremburg war trials a witness was called upon to give evidence. He had lived for some time in a Jewish cemetery in Wilna, Poland. He had miraculously escaped the Nazi gas chambers by hiding in the cemetery. There were others who had also made the cemetery their secret hiding place. One day, he related, a woman gave birth to an infant boy in an open grave. The old Jewish grave digger, eighty years old, assisted at the birth. When the newborn baby uttered his first cry, the devout old grave digger said, "Good God, hast Thou finally sent Messiah to us? For who else than the Messiah Himself can be born in a grave?" But after three days he saw that the baby was sucking his mother's tears because she had no milk for him. [5]

It is a story of profound poignancy, of moving emotional power. And yet we forget the harrowing truth that the Son of God, the Messiah, was born two thousand years ago in an animal's feeding trough, in the stench of an Eastern stable, and that He died in naked loneliness and dereliction upon a cruel cross, having drunk to the bitter dregs the cup of human tears.

The remembrance of this fact should humble our pride.

[4] *The Brothers Karamazov,* Part II, Book V.
[5] Paul Tillich, *The Shaking of the Foundations* (New York: C. Scribner's Sons, 1948), p. 165.

It should move us to penitence. "... he was wounded for our transgressions," writes the prophet Isaiah, "he was bruised for our iniquities; upon him was the chastisement that made us whole, and with his stripes we are healed" (Isaiah 53:5). It is the recollection of this fact that should evoke our gratitude and win our love and inspire our service.

This truth is memorably expressed in the haunting words of a 17th century hymn, the *Hymn of St. Francis Xavier,* translated from the Latin by Edward Caswall:

> My God, I love Thee — not because
> I hope for heaven thereby,
> Nor yet because who love Thee not
> Are lost eternally.

> Thou, O my Jesus, Thou didst me
> Upon the Cross embrace;
> For me didst bear the nails and spear,
> And manifold disgrace,

> And griefs and torments numberless,
> And sweat of agony,
> And death itself — and all for me,
> Who was Thine enemy.

> Then why, O blessed Jesus Christ,
> Should I not love Thee well?
> Not for the sake of winning heaven,
> Nor of escaping hell;

> Not with the hope of gaining aught;
> Nor seeking a reward;
> But as Thyself hast loved me,
> O ever-loving Lord.

> E'en so I love Thee, and will love,
> And in Thy praise will sing;
> Because Thou art my loving God,
> And my eternal King.

Chapter Four

ONE OF THE CROWD

"A crowd being anonymous, and in consequence irresponsible," writes Gustave le Bon, "the sentiment of responsibility which controls individuals disappears entirely." [1] Kierkegaard says the same thing. In a crowd, he points out, men become "impenitent and irresponsible," capable of any devilry, of any brutality.

Rabble rousers know this elementary fact. All that is required, Kierkegaard suggests, is "some talent, a certain dose of falsehood, and a little acquaintance with human passions." The rest is easy.

Aldous Huxley asserts that the appeal of a crowd is basically orgiastic and Dionysian. The experience of being absorbed in a crowd, he suggests, is remarkably akin to alcoholic intoxication. There is the same sense of emotional release, of ecstatic exitement, of uninhibited freedom. "Most human beings," he explains, "feel a craving to escape from the cramping limitations of their ego, to take periodical holidays from their all too familiar, all too squalid little self." [2] And this escape from the restrictions of the self is most simply and easily achieved in the safe anonymity of the crowd. "The truth is," Kierkegaard adds, "that in the herd we are free from the standard of the individual and the ideal."

[1] *The Crowd* (New York: The Viking Press, 1760), p. 30. Quoted by permission.

[2] *Ends and Means* (New York: Harper and Bros., 1937), p. 80.

I

Mass sports are the characteristic feature of a civilization in the ripeness of decay. The Roman civilization, in the first century of the Christian era, found it necessary to sustain its waning life-sense by the provision of gladiatorial shows of increasing barbarity. The proletarian population of Rome was not content with bread: it wanted, not only bread, but also circuses. Pompey was the first, we are told, to introduce combat between men and animals. It is related that Claudius' special delight at the gladiatorial shows was in watching the countenances of the dying, for he had learned to take an artistic pleasure in studying their agony.

Fresh devices were conceived to stimulate the flagging interest of jaded spirits. Nero illumined his gardens at night by burning Christians smeared in pitch as living torches.

"The magnificent circus," Lecky writes, "the gorgeous dresses of the assembled Court, the contagion of a passionate enthusiasm thrilling almost visibly through the mighty throng, the breathless silence of expectation, the wild cheers bursting simultaneously from eighty thousand tongues, and echoing to the farthest outskirts of the city, the rapid alternations of the fray, the deeds of splendid courage that were manifested, were all well fitted to entrance the imagination." [3]

A few lone voices were raised in impotent protest. Seneca denounced the games with passionate eloquence. He declared that such amusements were brutalizing, savage, and detestable. Plutarch argued that the sight of blood and of suffering is necessarily and essentially depraving and that, in any case, we should have a bond of sympathy with all sentient beings.

II

Lewis Mumford draws attention to the fact that mass sports play an indispensible role in the life of the average

[3] W. E. H. Lecky, *History of European Morals from Augustus to Charlemagne* (New York: Longmans, Green & Co., 1911), Volume 1, p. 282.

man. "Sport, in the sense of a mass spectacle, with death to add to the underlying excitement, comes into existence," he observes, "when a population has been drilled and regimented and depressed to such an extent that it needs at least a vicarious participation in difficult feats of skill or heroism to sustain its waning life-sense." [4]

Mass sports not only arouse emotion, they provide an opportunity for its controlled expression and relief. The thrill of the spectacle is intensified by the promise of immediate death or fatal injury. Lewis Mumford writes,

> The cry of horror that escapes from the crowd when the motor car overturns or the airplane crashes is not one of surprise, but of fulfilled expectation; is it not fundamentally for the sake of exciting just such bloodlust that the competition itself is held and widely attended? By means of the talking picture that spectacle and that thrill are repeated in a thousand theatres throughout the world as a mere incident in the presentation of the week's news; so that a steady habituation to blood-letting and exhibitionistic murder and suicide accompanies the spread of the machine and, becoming stale by the repetition in its milder forms, encourages the demand for more massive and desperate exhibitions of brutality. [5]

In the midst of the crowd, the spectator shares in these exploits by means of psychological projection and self-identification. He becomes

> at one with a primitive undifferentiated group. His muscles contract or relax with the progress of the game, his breath comes quick or slow, his shouts heighten the excitement of the moment and increase his internal sense of the drama: in moments of frenzy he pounds his neighbor's back or embraces him. [6]

All this is a matter of common observation.

Augustine, in his *Confessions*, illustrates the nature of the phenomenon by reference to the experience of his close

[4] *Op. cit.,* p. 303.
[5] *Ibid,* p. 304.
[6] *Ibid,* p. 305.

friend, Alypius. Alypius, vigorously protesting, was forcibly carried off to a gladiatorial combat. He vehemently insisted that while they could compel his body they could not compel his mind. When they were seated, he fixed his mind on other matters and kept his eyes tightly shut. Unluckily not his ears, for, as Augustine relates,

> when, on the fall of one of the fighters, a great shout from all the spectators smote him, he opened his eyes — to be worse wounded in soul than the fighter he was impelled to look at was in body . . . . For along with the sight of the blood-covered man he took in a dose of savagery, and, instead of turning away, fixed his gaze, and willy-nilly drank up the horrors, delighting in the shocking sight and intoxicated with the bloodthirsty pleasure. He was no longer what he was when he came, but was now just one of the crowd . . . . He watched, shouted, was inflamed, and went away with a mania that forced him to return, and to do so not only with those who had dragged him there but even ahead of them and himself dragging others. [7]

III

Modern dictators have skillfully exploited the emotional frustrataion of proletarian man for their own selfish purposes. They have discovered that, by means of mammoth rallies, it is easy to excite and foment the animal passions of hate and fear that are latent within us all. They have learned that in a crowd a man is willing to surrender himself to "the darkness of sub-human emotionalism and panic animality." In a crowd, le Bon repeats, a man "is no longer himself, but has become an automaton who has ceased to be guided by his will." [8] He is no longer rational and responsible; he has become a demagogue's dupe.

William Sargent, in his disturbing book, *Battle for the Mind,* draws attention to the fact that there are now new and previously unheard of devices with which to achieve the subversion of the mind. Through the raucous voice of

[7] Book VI.
[8] *Op. cit.,* p. 32.

the demagogue, through heady music, through herd intoxication, it is possible to reduce a man, he points out, to a state of mindless subhumanity.

IV

Unhappily, this phenomenon is no new discovery. On Palm Sunday Jesus was joyfully acclaimed by the crowd as the promised Messiah:

> Most of the crowd spread their garments on the road, and others cut branches from the trees and spread them on the road. And the crowds that went before him and that followed him shouted, "Hosanna to the Son of David! Blessed be he who comes in the name of the Lord! Hosanna in the highest!" (Matthew 21:8, 9).

And yet, five days later that same crowd, at the instigation of the Jewish leaders, was howling for His blood. It is always the fickle crowd which, in its blind ignorance, shouts: "Crucify Him! Crucify Him!" Such is the cruel irresponsibility, the basic irrationality, of the crowd.

Jesus, knowing that the crowd, in Kierkegaard's emphatic words, is untruth, refused to use the weapons of the world and the devices of the demagogue in the service of truth. After the feeding of the five thousand, when the crowd was eager to make Him a King, He significantly "withdrew again to the hills by himself" (John 6:15). He refused to encourage their dangerous and self-destructive hysteria.

V

Jesus formed His followers into a community and a church. There is a fundamental difference between a crowd and a community. In a crowd a man's personality is obliterated by its submersion in the mass; in a community, through the experience of fellowship, a man's personality is enriched and enhanced. In a crowd, there is only the possibility of anonymous animality; in a community, there are rich opportunities for the expression of individuality and what Alec Vidler, in

an arresting phrase, calls "exciting eccentricity." [9]   "Gregar-
iousness," Boris Pasternak acutely suggests, "is always the
refuge of mediocrities; only individuals seek the truth."

[9] *Theology* (London: S. P. C. K.), June, 1961, p. 221.

Chapter Five

THE ENIGMA OF DEATH

In popular mythology death has always been portrayed as a hideous skeleton with empty eye sockets and a long inexorable finger summoning man, refusing to be denied. In Lucerne there is a bridge known as the Bridge of Death. In every panel of the bridge there is a picture of death breaking into life. Death comes to the soldier, the statesman, the merchant, the beggar, he comes to all and he comes to each; he comes, a grisly apparition filling the heart with dismay.

By contrast, the Christian man is able to face death without fear. Dr. Edward Wilson was a member of Captain Scott's fateful Antarctic Expedition. Dr. Wilson was the medical officer of the Expedition, and he was among the picked band which reached the South Pole. It was on the return journey that the members of the advance party were overwhelmed with disaster. They were caught in a fearful blizzard which raged without intermission day after day. One by one they succumbed to the appalling rigors of frostbite and cold. Only Captain Scott and Edward Wilson were left alive. Isolated from their supplies, snowbound within their tent, they knew there was no possibility of survival. Wilson's farewell letter to his wife was found months later on his frozen body, together with his Bible and with his Prayer Book. This is what he wrote:

To My Beloved Wife. Don't be unhappy — all is for the best. We are playing a good part in a great scheme arranged by God Himself, and all is well . . . . We will all meet after death and death has no terrors. . . . All is for the best to those that love God, and oh, my Ory, we have both loved Him with all our lives. All is well . . . My beloved wife . . . life itself is a small thing to me now, but my love for you is for ever and a part of our love for God. I do not cease to pray for you and to desire that you may be filled with the knowledge of His will. (Later) All the things I had hoped to do with you after the Expedition are as nothing now, but there are greater things for us to do in the world to come . . . . Your little testament and prayer book will be in my hand or in my breast pocket when the end comes. All is well. . . [1]

These deeply poignant words of Edward Wilson reveal something of the simple and sincere faith which animated and sustained him. He was a man of transparent sincerity and earnest faith — he was a man who trusted in God and who sought to serve Him — and, as a consequence, he was able to face death without fear. His last words breathe a spirit of quiet serenity and of confident trust.

I

It is impressive to note how often Christian martyrs invoke the metaphor of marriage to describe the transition of death. On the evening before his martyrdom Bishop Nicholas Ridley invited his keeper's wife, and others at the table, to his marriage: "for," said he, "tomorrow I must be married, and so showed himself to be as merry as ever he had been before."

Sir Thomas Herbert tells us that Charles I went forth to his execution with the gay exhilaration of a bridegroom going forth to meet his bride: "This is my second Marriage Day; I would be as trim today as may be; for before night I hope to be espoused to my blessed Jesus." And then he added: "Death is not terrible to me. I bless my God I am prepared." [2]

[1] George Seaver, *Edward Wilson of the Antarctic* (New York: Transatlantic Arts, 1946), pp. 293-4.
[2] *The Trial of Charles I*, a contemporary account taken from the memoirs of Sir Thomas Herbert and John Ruskworth. Edited by Roger Lockyer. (London: The Folio Society, 1959) p. 126.

The natural man knows nothing about this assurance of a blessed immortality. For him, as John Donne reminds us, "death is a bloody conflict, and no victory at last; a tempestuous sea, and no harbour at last; a slippery height and no footing; a desperate fall and no bottom." [3]

For the Christian man death is, in the exultant words of Dietrich Bonhoeffer, "the supreme festival on the road to freedom": [4] an occasion for joyous thanksgiving and confident rejoicing.

II

"Death," Aristotle confesses, "is a dreadful thing, for it is the end." Thomas Hobbes confides: "I am about to take my last voyage, a great leap in the dark." "He who pretends to face death without fear," Rousseau bluntly affirms, "is a liar." "No rational man," Dr. Johnson insists, "can die without uneasy apprehension." "We live in a crowd," Robert McKenna notes, "but we die alone." Heidegger says the same thing: "Dying my death is the one thing nobody else can do for me."

T. S. Eliot likens the way men die to the whimpering of a dying dog:

> This is the way the world ends,
> This is the way the world ends,
> This is the way the world ends,
> Not with a bang but a whimper. [5]

For the Christian man the last word is not with the grave but with God: that is why there is no whimpering and no whining, no repining and no complaining. That is why the Christian man is able to say, with the Shepherd Psalmist: "Even though I walk through the valley of the shadow of death, I fear no evil; for thou art with me" (Psalm 23:4). "For I am sure," the Apostle Paul confidently affirms, "that

[3] *The Sermons of John Donne*, selected and introduced by Theodore Gill (New York: Meridian Books, 1958) p. 233.

[4] *Letters and Papers from Prison*, edited by Eberhard Bethge and translated by Reginald H. Fuller (London: S.C.M. Press, 1953), p. 176. Quoted by permission.

[5] "The Hollow Men," in *Complete Poems & Plays* by T. S. Eliot (New York: Harcourt, Brace and Co., 1962).

neither death, nor life . . . will be able to separate us from
the love of God in Christ Jesus our Lord" (Romans 8:38, 39).

III

Boris Pasternak, the celebrated Russian writer, in his
Nobel Prize winning novel, *Doctor Zhivago,* refers to "the
centuries of systematic work devoted to the solution of the
enigma of death, so that death itself may eventually be
overcome." [6]
For the Christian man death is not an enigma, but an
enemy, an enemy whose power has been broken and whose
sting has been removed. "Jesus," the Apostle Paul triumphantly affirmed, ". . . abolished death and brought life and
immortality to light through the gospel" (II Timothy 1:10).
It is sin, the apostle explains, that gives to death its sting.
It is the consciousness of guilt that makes a man afraid. It
is the anxious uncertainty of that which lies on the other
side of death, the secret fear of punishment, that fills a man
with apprehensive dread.
The Christian man, however, is able to face death with
a quiet conscience and a sure hope: a quiet conscience, because he knows that on the cross his sins were pardoned
and forgiven; a sure hope, because he knows that Jesus has
risen from the dead. Death, for the Christian man, is a de-
feated foe: "O death," the apostle demands, "where is thy
victory? O death, where is thy sting?" And then he adds,
with joyous exultation: "But thanks be to God, who gives
us the victory through our Lord Jesus Christ" (I Corinthians
15:55, 57).
We can illustrate what this means, from the point of view
of contemporary man, by reference to a remarkable collection
of letters, written by men on the eve of their execution at
the hands of the Nazis, edited by Trevor Huddleston and entitled *Dying We Live.* Christoph Probst, a student of the
University of Munich, was executed by the firing squad on
February 22, 1943 for promoting opposition to the Nazi State.
Prior to his execution, he wrote to his mother:

[6] (New York: New American Library, Inc., 1958), p. 19.

I thank you for having given me life. When I really think it through, it has all been a single road to God. Do not grieve that I must now skip the last part of it. Soon I shall be closer to you than before. In the meantime I'll prepare a glorious reception for you all.

And to his sister:

I never knew that dying is so easy . . . I die without any feeling or hatred . . . Never forget that life is nothing but a growing in love and a preparation for eternity. [7]

Hermann Stohr, writing to his sister, gives a like testimony:

For me as for others it holds true that Christ has freed us from the fear of death, and that perfect love drives out fear. Perfect love — that is HE. And he may draw us all into this love. And once we stand within it, all suffering must vanish for us, and we shall partake of great joy. Whatever we have to reproach one another for, let us forgive completely with the petition of the Lord's Prayer: "Our Father . . . forgive us our trespasses, as we forgive those who trespass against us." — And let us go thus to meet the day that will unite us all in eternity. [8]

IV

What Christians affirm is that Jesus, on the cross, accomplished (in the classic words of W. Williams) "the death of death and hell's destruction."

"Since therefore the children share in flesh and blood," the writer of the epistle to the Hebrews explains, "he himself likewise partook of the same nature, that through death he might destroy him who has the power of death, that is, the devil, and deliver all those who through fear of death were subject to lifelong bondage" (Hebrews 2:14, 15).

It is Christ's glorious victory which we celebrate on Easter Day. And, in the fruits of that victory, we share by faith. That is why we join the faithful down the ages, joyfully proclaiming:

[7] (New York: Collins, William, Sons & Company, 1958), pp. 57-8. Quoted by permission.
[8] *Ibid*, p. 185.

Alleluia! Alleluia! Alleluia!
The strife is o'er, the battle done;
Now is the Victor's triumph won;
O let the song of praise be sung.
                    Alleluia!
Death's mightiest powers have done their worst,
And Jesus hath his foes dispersed;
Let shouts of praise and joy outburst:
                    Alleluia!
He closed the yawning gates of hell,
The bars from heaven's high portals fell;
Let songs of praise his triumph tell!
                    Alleluia!
On the third morn he rose again,
Glorious in majesty to reign;
O let us swell the joyful strain.
                    Alleluia!
Lord, by the stripes which wounded thee,
From death's dread sting thy servants free,
That we may live, and sing to thee.
                    Alleluia!

Chapter Six

WHAT'S IN A NAME?

Dr. Samuel Johnson enjoys the distinction of having completed the first English Dictionary. It is a tribute to his astonishing industry that, unaided, he brought this exacting enterprise to a successful and triumphant conclusion.

Initially, he sought the patronage of Lord Chesterfield. His request was ignored. When the work was almost complete, and the nature of Johnson's achievement apparent, Lord Chesterfield was eager to offer the support he had previously withheld. Johnson, a proud and deeply sensitive man, satirically scorned the offer of belated assistance:

> Seven years, my Lord, have now passed, since I waited in your outward rooms, or was repulsed from your door; during which time I have been pushing on my work through difficulties of which it is useless to complain, and have brought it, at last, to the verge of publication, without one act of assistance, one word of encouragement, or one smile of favour. Such treatment I did not expect, for I never had a patron before . . .
>
> Is not a Patron, my Lord, one who looks with unconcern on a man struggling in the water, and, when he has reached ground, encumbers him with help? The notice which you have been pleased to take of my labours, had it been early, had been kind; but it has been delayed till I am indifferent, and cannot enjoy it; till I am solitary, and cannot impart it; till I am known, and do not want it. I hope it is no very cynical asperity, not to confess obligations where no benefit has been received, or to be unwilling that the Public should

45

consider me as owing that to a Patron which Providence has enabled me to do for myself.

Having carried on my work thus far with so little obligation to any favourer of learning, I shall not be disappointed though I should conclude it, if less be possible, with less; for I have been long awakened from that dream of hope, in which I once boasted myself, with so much exultation . . . My Lord, Your Lordship's most humble, most obedient servant.

Johnson was a pioneer in the science of lexicography and we tend to forget the cost that he paid in blood, toil, tears, and sweat.

Now there are dictionaries ranging from astronomy to zoology. One of the more recent, edited by Miss Withycombe and entitled, *The Oxford Dictionary of English Christian Names*, contains a wealth of fascinating detail about periodic fashions in given names. In the twelfth century the most common boys' names were William, Robert, and Richard. At that time only two per cent of the male population was called John. In the thirteenth century, however, John had risen so much in favor that no less than a quarter of the entire male population was called John. At all times the most popular girls' names have been Mary, Anne, Elizabeth, Joan, and Margaret. Strange names like Extranea, Hodierna, Melodia, and Splendor have enjoyed a brief popularity. The Puritans preferred Biblical names: names like Saul and Samuel, Deborah, Leah, and Rachel. They also coined a variety of other names, both strange and wonderful, such as Praise-God Barebones. Camden, in his *Remaines*, published in 1605, cites such names as Free-Gift, Earth, Dust, Ashes, Tribulation, The Lord is Near, and More Trial. One Parish *Register* records the name Sorry for Sin; another, No Merit; yet another, under date 1644, the one of a foundling girl, Misericordia Adulterina.

We might dismiss all this as a matter of antiquarian interest, and impatiently ask: "What's in a name?"

I

A man's name is, to begin with, a badge of identity. My name distinguishes me from Tom and Dick and Harry; it marks me out from all other men as *this* man rather than as *that* man; it separates me from all other men in the solitariness of my own individuality. My name gives me personal identity: it affirms that I am not simply one of the crowd, anonymous, without a name, submerged in the generality of men; it proclaims that I am *this* individual man, to be distinguished from every other by my possession of a name.

James Baldwin adopts the poignant title, *Nobody Knows My Name,* for a volume of his collected essays. For too long Negroes have known the bitter indignity of simply being addressed as "nigger" or "boy" or "you." We know that a man's name is not a matter of indifference, and that, for the Negro, as for all men, the achievement of status and dignity is dependent upon the possession of a name.

In James Joyce's semi-autobiographical novel, *The Portrait of an Artist as a Young Man,* Stephen Dedalus is angry and humiliated because the Jesuit Supervisor of Studies does not bother to remember his name. Father Dolan has twice asked his name. Stephen

> thought of the baldy head of the prefect of studies with the cruel noncoloured eyes looking at him and he heard the voice of the prefect of studies asking him twice what his name was. Why could he not remember the name when he was told the first time? Was he not listening the first time or was it to make fun out of the name? The great men of history had names like that and nobody made fun of them. It was his own name that he should have made fun of if he wanted to make fun. Dolan: it was like the name of a woman that washed clothes. [1]

To Stephen, as to every man, his name is a matter of profound personal importance; that is why he regards it as a grave and calculated affront that Father Dolan continues to forget it.

[1] *Portrait of the Artist as a Young Man* (New York: Viking Press, 1964), p. 55.

In the more ancient English Public Schools, it was, for many years, a tradition to distinguish boys of the same name by the convenient expedient of temporal seniority. Teachers simply spoke of Smith major, Smith minor, or Smith minimus, as the case might be. This practice has gradually been abandoned for something less impersonal: the custom is now to address the boy by his initials as Smith A. B., or Smith P. T., or Smith J. D.; not, of course, anything so disconcertingly personal, so embarrassingly intimate, as a boy's given name. Nevertheless, at long last, in the safe citadels of English conservativism, boys are no longer categorized as larger or smaller specimens of the species Smith of the genus man.

A man's name, then, is a badge of identity. Illegitimate children are often burdened with a deep sense of personal insecurity, because they do not know their name, and, therefore, their true identity. The latest biographer of T. E. Lawrence of Arabia believes that this is the key to the perplexing enigma of his character. He was the illegitimate son of an Irish baronet. His strange and restless life was, among other things, the search for a name and therefore for identity. This explains why it was that at one time he adopted the name of Ross and, at another time, the name of Shaw.

God, in our redemption, recognizes our identity as distinct and distinguishable persons. God addresses us, saying: "I have called you by name." There is, as Francis Thompson rightly reminds us:

> . . . no expeditious road
> To pack and label men for God,
> And save them by the barrel-load.

No! there is only the personal word, addressed not to the many but to the one, the saving word addressed to each: "Fear not, for I have redeemed you; I have called you *by name*, you are mine" (Isaiah 43:1).

II

A man's name, however, is not only a badge of identity, it is also a badge of character.

Jacob was a liar and a cheat, one who double-crossed his

father and deceived his brother. He was thus appropriately named Jacob: one who supplants. There was something strangely prophetic about the fact that, in the very act of being born, he took his brother's heel by the hand. He was rightly named Jacob because he was a sharp, calculating and unscrupulous trickster. He was, God testified, a worm (Isaiah 41:14). The name Jacob aptly described his character. In old age, however, Jacob sought God in penitence and prayer. In a decisive moment he came face to face with God and, in that never-to-be-forgotten encounter, he became a changed man. He was then given a new name to signify his new character: Israel, a Prince with God. In the book of Revelation we read that those who triumph in Christ over the Evil One will also be given a new name (Revelation 2: 17).

A man's name is a badge of character: that is why, in ordinary conversation, when we speak of a man's good name, we mean his character. Every self-respecting man takes pride in having a good name. Tennyson calls slander "the meanest spawn of hell." By deliberate misrepresentation, by whispered innuendo, by subtle suggestion, the foul work of defamation is done: a man's good name is smeared and smutted, his character is impugned and his reputation is destroyed. Iago is speaking the truth, in spite of himself, when he protests:

> Who steals my purse steals trash; 'tis something, nothing:
> 'Twas mine, 'tis his, and has been slave to thousands;
> But he that filches from me my good name
> Robs me of that which not enriches him,
> And makes me poor indeed.

Every right-thinking man is jealous for his good name; that is why God is jealous for His good name. The third commandment warns against taking God's name in vain: "You shall not take the name of the Lord your God in vain; for the Lord will not hold him guiltless who takes his name in vain" (Exodus 20:7). When we invoke the name of God we invoke God. To take God's name in vain — to invoke God

casually and carelessly — is to mock Him and to deride Him.
The Jews, for their part, were fearful of such dreadful blas-
phemy. No Jew would presume to write the holy name of
God without preparatory ceremonial ablutions — scrupulous-
ly washing his arm to the elbow and then using a new pen
or a new quill. When reading the sacred Scriptures no Jew
would presume to utter the ineffable name of God lest he
incur the dreadful sin of sacrilege: instead, he substituted
the periphrasis, "the Name." A consequence of this is that
we no longer know the correct pronunciation for the name of
God: whether it was Jehovah or Jahweh or Jahve: the fact
is that it was never spoken lest it be spoken in vain.

III

When the Son of God was born he was given a name de-
scriptive of His work. " . . . you shall call his name Jesus,"
(the name means "Saviour," "the one who saves") the angel
explained, "for he will save his people from their sins" (Matthew 1:21).

That is why the name of Jesus is precious beyond comparison: it speaks both of His Person and His work. John
Newton reminds us of what the name of Jesus means in saving power:

>How sweet the Name of Jesus sounds
>In a believer's ear!
>It soothes his sorrows, heals his wounds,
>And drives away his fear.
>
>It makes the wounded spirit whole,
>And calms the troubled breast;
>'Tis manna to the hungry soul,
>And to the weary rest.
>
>Dear Name! the rock on which I build,
>My shield, and hiding-place,
>My never-failing treasury, filled
>With boundless stores of grace!
>
>Jesus, my Shepherd, Brother, Friend,
>My Prophet, Priest, and King,
>My Lord, my Life, my Way, my End,
>Accept the praise I bring.

Weak is the effort of my heart
  And cold my warmest thought;
But when I see Thee as Thou art
  I'll praise Thee as I ought.

Till then I would Thy love proclaim
  With every fleeting breath;
And may the music of Thy Name
  Refresh my soul in death.

The man in the street knows nothing of the efficacious significance of the name of Jesus. It is hidden from him. For him the name of Jesus is simply an overworked expletive, a meaningless ejaculation, a blasphemous oath.

Bernard of Clairvaux speaks ecstatically of what the name of Jesus means.

> As honey to the taste, as melody in the ear, as songs of gladness in the heart, so is the name of Jesus . . . . Naught but the name of Jesus can restrain the impulse of anger, repress the swelling of pride, cure the wound of envy, bridle the onslaught of luxury, extinguish the flame of carnal desire — can temper avarice, and put to flight impure and ignoble thoughts. For when I name the name of Jesus, I call to mind at once a Man meek and lowly of heart, benign, pure, temperate, merciful; a Man conspicuous for every honourable and saintly quality; and also in the same Person the Almighty God — so that He both restores me to health by His example and renders me strong by His assistance. No less than this is brought to my mind by the name of Jesus whenever I hear it.

For the Christian man the name of Jesus is "above every name": it is peerless and pre-eminent, sacred and sublime. Jesus is the Saviour, the same yesterday, today, and forever. In this He differs from every earthly saviour. On the cross He saved men from their sins, and He saves them still. This is His prerogative and His gift. As John Donne once said: "Caesar is not Caesar still nor Alexander, Alexander, but Jesus is Jesus still, and shall be forever."

Chapter Seven

THE LAST REFUGE OF A SCOUNDREL?

It is fashionable to decry patriotism as a prejudice and a sin. Grant Allen calls it "a vulgar vice," and Havelock Ellis defines it as "a virtue among barbarians." "Patriotism," Ruskin repeats, "is an absurd prejudice, founded on an extended selfishness." [1] "Patriotism," according to Dr. Johnson, "is the last refuge of a scoundrel." [2]

In this twentieth century the denigration of patriotism has proceeded apace. During the inter-war years the undergraduates of the University of Oxford passed a notorious resolution affirming that under no circumstances would they fight for King and Country. G. K. Chesterton was moved to protest:

> I am all the more anxious to avert such a disaster falling again upon the world, now that I know that my friends and brethren are henceforth doomed to suffer twice for the crime of patriotism; to be destroyed by their enemies and then despised by their countrymen. [3]

Is there still a place for patriotism? Or is patriotism a relic of the past, an atavistic survival, an unhappy anachronism,

[1] Quoted, W. R. Inge, *Outspoken Essays* (London: Longmans, Green, 1920), p. 35.

[2] James Boswell, *Life of Johnson,* 7 April, 1775.

[3] This, of course, is no new thing. Francis Quarles (1592-1644) wrote:

> Our God and soldier we alike adore,
> When at the brink of ruin, not before;
> After deliv'rance both alike requited,
> Our God forgotten, and our soldiers slighted.

Human behaviour is depressingly predictable.

a crude and barbaric thing? Is there a place for a patriotism which is at once humble and honorable, or is patriotism only a vulgar vice — egoism, magnified and disguised?

I

In the first place, we need to define more precisely what we mean by patriotism.

There is a form of patriotism which is blatantly jingoistic, a patriotism which is militant, pugnacious, and self-righteous. Disraeli, at the Congress of Berlin, was guilty of shameless saber rattling; it was reflected in the popular music hall refrain:

> We don't want to fight
> But, by jingo if we do,
> We've got the ships, we've got the men,
> We've got the money too.

This kind of patriotism — bloated with pride and swollen with egoism — is deplorable. It is arrogant and aggressive; its offense is rank, it smells to heaven; it invites and deserves the judgment of God.

Nations which are powerful and mighty are necessarily exposed to great temptation. They are tempted to insolence and pride, to despise (in Kipling's phrase) the "lesser breeds without the Law." Milton was of the opinion that when the Almighty has something unusually great or difficult to be done, He entrusts it, as His manner is, first to His Englishmen. [4] But this is a dangerous delusion and a foolish conceit. No nation dare assume that it is the privileged recipient of the Almighty's exclusive favors. We rightly reject doctrines of racial superiority as the paranoid product of a diseased imagination; we need to beware of perpetrating the same error under the guise of a blind and passionate patriotism.

II

But there is another kind of patriotism which is neither boastful nor bombastic — a patriotism which is humble and devoid of conceit.

[4] *Areopagitica*

A patriot, from this point of view, is one who has an earnest concern for the true welfare of his country. Believing that "righteousness exalts a nation, but [that] sin is a reproach to any people" (Proverbs 14:34) he does not close his eyes to those things which are wrong, but he sees, in imagination, his country as it ought to be — dedicated to the service of righteousness and truth. He does not say, arrogantly, with Stephen Decatur: " . . . our country, right or wrong"; on the contrary, he says, with Richard Lovelace:

> I could not love thee, dear, so much,
> Lov'd I not honour more.

A patriot, then, is one who has a passionate dedication to the right and an earnest desire to promote it. To abstain from making moral judgments is not patriotism but treachery. As Aaron Henry recently reminded us, in relation to those racial problems that plague us, "it is not the noise of the bad, but the thundering silence of the good people, that causes so much trouble." The man who fails to speak out in the presence of evil is failing both as a citizen and as a patriot, for, by his silence, he lends consent.

The true patriot is not concerned whether God is on his side but he is deeply concerned as to whether his country is on the side of God. During the dark days of the Civil War a clergyman, talking to Lincoln, expressed the pious hope that "the Lord was on our side." Lincoln replied: "I am not at all concerned about that, for I know that the Lord is *always* on the side of the *right*. But it is my constant anxiety and prayer that *I* and *this nation* should be on the Lord's side." [5] Because a patriot loves his country he loves other things more — things which alone can make a country great — justice, righteousness, and truth. "For what," Jesus asked, "does it profit a man, to gain the whole world and forfeit his life? For what can a man give in return for his life?" (Mark 8:36, 37).

---

[5] Quoted, William J. Wolf, *The Religion of Abraham Lincoln* (New York: Seabury, 1963), p. 128.

III

Too often patriotism has been a patent mask for egoism. It was this fact which provoked Samuel Johnson to conclude that patriotism is the last refuge of a scoundrel. "He did not mean," James Boswell hastens to add, by way of qualification, "a real and generous love of country, but that pretended patriotism which so many, in all ages and countries, have made a cloak for self interest." [6]

There is, H. G. Wells warns, a crazy combative patriotism abroad in the world today that plainly threatens to destroy civilization. "Patriotism," Bolingbroke insists, "must be founded in great principles and supported by great virtues." Otherwise it will degenerate into an immoral obsession and become an appalling perversion. Nurse Edith Cavell was sensitively aware that patriotism is not enough. As she faced the firing squad she said: "I must have no hatred or bitterness towards anyone."

Bishop Berkeley rightly observes:

> Whatever the world thinks, he who hath not much meditated upon God, the human mind, and the *Summum Bonum*, may possibly make a thriving earthworm, but will indubitably make a sorry patriot and a sorry statesman.

The heart of man, Calvin charges, is a great idol factory. Herbert Butterfield argues that we have replaced idols of wood and stone with a modern idolatry of abstract nouns. Apart from faith in God, patriotism, as Bishop Berkeley observes, is, at the best, a sorry thing, at the worst, an immoral obsession. Pride, it has been said, ends in narcissism, and patriotism, if not chastened and contrite, ends in idolatry. Denis de Rougemont acutely observes that Eros only ceases to be a devil when it ceases to be a god, and the same may be said of patriotism. We dare not give to any earthly thing that loyalty which properly belongs to God.

[6] *Ibid.*

IV

We urgently need a revival of true patriotism — a patriotism which is neither bellicose nor belligerent — a patriotism which is pure and without offense. We need a patriotism which is both humble and devout — the kind of patriotism to which Lincoln appealed when he said: "With malice towards none; with charity for all; with firmness in the right as God gives us to see the right, let us strive on to finish the work we are in. . . ."

Patriotism, properly understood, is a single-minded dedication to the pursuit of that which is right. "What do we mean by patriotism in the context of our lives?" Adlai Stevenson asked, and he answered his own question: We mean "a patriotism which is not frenzied outbursts of emotion, but the tranquil and steady dedication of a lifetime." [7] Without the enabling grace of God, however, our dedication is likely to be neither tranquil nor steady, but, too often, frenzied and hysteric. Apart from God, our very virtues tend to become vices. To avoid the corruption and perversion of that which is good we need to beware of that pride which goes before a fall. "He has showed you, O man, what is good; and what does the Lord require of you but to do justice, and to love kindness, and to walk humbly with your God?" (Micah 6:8).

[7] Speech. New York City, 27 August, 1952.

Chapter Eight

THE BALCONY APPROACH TO LIFE

In 1939 an American submarine was sunk in 180 feet of water. At that time that was the greatest depth at which salvage operations could be undertaken. The task was entrusted to a young lieutenant. The assignment proved one of unusual difficulty. Not only was there the depth at which the work had to be done, with its tremendous water pressure, but weather conditions were unexpectedly adverse. Winter was approaching, and, as the weather steadily deteriorated, the decision was made to suspend further operations until the following spring. The lieutenant decided that, if the job was to be done, he must know more about the dangers and difficulties of the task. So, during the winter months, he learned the art of diving. When spring came, and operations were resumed, he resolved that he would be the first to go over the side. He donned his diving suit, the helmet was placed in position, the bolts were fastened, and then — his feet weighted with lead — he was lowered over the side of the ship into that realm of perpetual darkness down below. No sooner had his feet touched the bottom of the ocean floor that he was seized with a feeling of intolerable nausea, a sense of terrifying claustrophobia, as though he would suffocate beneath the waves. Frantically he put out his hand to pull the life-line to signal those above to haul him to the surface. And then, by an act of almost superhuman will power, he steeled himself and determined that come what may, he would do his full spell of duty down below. After what seemed an eternity of time the signal came from above that his time was up. He was hauled to the surface; the bolts were unfastened, his helmet was removed, and he was released from his diving suit. After that inauspicious beginning, he found that it was not so difficult, after all, to take his turn on the roster. At last the job was done: the submarine was salvaged and the men were paid off. As they were leaving, the mate of the ship said to the lieutenant: "You know, Sir, there is not a man on this ship who wouldn't go through hell for you."

There is, of course, all the difference in the world between the man who stays on the bridge and the man who plunges into the depths; between the lieutenant who, from the safe security of the bridge, projects his tender sympathy to his men struggling below, and that same lieutenant, one with them, sharing their dangers, their difficulties, and their final success.

I

There are, John Mackay suggests, two approaches to life: what he calls the balcony approach and the approach from the road.

In Spanish American countries, it is customary to build houses with balconies or platforms projecting from the upper window of the second floor.

The balcony symbolizes the spectator approach to life; the approach from the road suggests, by contrast, the way of the pilgrim. John Mackay explains:

> The Balcony is the symbol of the perfect spectator for whom life and the universe are permanent objects of study and contemplation. . . . By the Road I mean the place where life is tensely lived, where thought has its birth in conflict and concern, where choices are made and decisions are carried out. It is the place of action, of pilgrimage, of crusade, where concern is never absent from the wayfarer's heart. On the Road a goal is sought, dangers are faced, life is poured out. . . . The Road, like the Balcony, is a state of Soul. [1]

[1] *A Preface to Christian Theology* (New York: Macmillan, 1942), p. 29. Quoted by permission.

II

The difference between these two different philosophies of life may be illustrated by reference to Ernest Renan and Father Damien.

Ernest Renan, a French sceptic, was the author of a famous life of Christ. "I would not like the world to be transformed," he writes, in one of his *Essays*, "because a reformed world would be so much less interesting." "If there should be a life to come," he confides, "I would ask the Eternal Father to give me a box seat in order that I might see the spectacle." [2]

Renan adopted the spectator attitude to life. He was unconcerned about the agonies and toils of suffering humanity; for him, life was a pageant to be watched, a spectacle to be enjoyed.

Father Damien adopted a very different point of view. He offered to serve the afflicted lepers on the island of Molokai in the Hawaiian Archipelago. In the dispensary, he ministered to their physical needs and, in the chapel, he sought to speak to them of the love of God. There came a day when he began his sermon with these words: "We lepers." They knew then that his identification with them had taken a more intimate and a more terrible form, and that he was now one with them in a solidarity of suffering.

Renan's attitude was one of supercilious superiority and aloof arrogance; Damien's, by contrast, was one of self-forgetful service and loving compassion. Renan was untouched by the needs of men, whereas Damien voluntarily took the sorrows and sufferings of men upon himself.

III

Behind these different philosophies of life there are two contrasted views of God.

To Aristotle God was the unmoved Mover, the sublime and dispassionate Spectator. It would derogate from His perfection, he said, to suggest that God might be interested

[2] Quoted, *ibid*, p. 31.

in the affairs of men; to suggest that He might be touched with the feeling of our infirmities, he argued, would imply insufficiency and imperfection.

Christians, by contrast, affirm God's active involvement and personal participation in the tragic affairs of men. ". . . he has borne our griefs and carried our sorrows," Isaiah says (Isaiah 53:4). "In all their affliction," the prophet repeats, "he was afflicted" (Isaiah 63:9).

It is not surprising that, whereas for the Epicurean, the supreme goal of life is *ataraxia* (freedom from fear, pain and passion) and for the Stoic *apatheia* (calm resignation), for the Christian, the supreme goal of life is *agape* (self-denying love) (John 3:16).

The Christian belief about God finds its final expression in the subduing declaration that "God was in Christ reconciling the world to himself . . . " (II Corinthians 5:19). "For our sake," Paul continues, "he made him to be sin who knew no sin, so that in him we might become the righteousness of God" (II Corinthians 5:21). Beza finely comments: "He was made what He is not (he made him to be sin who knew no sin) so that we (who are sinners) might be made what we are not (the righteousness of God in him)."

Jesus knew that He was called upon to fulfill a destiny of voluntary suffering and death. "I have a baptism to be baptized with," He testified, "and how I am constrained until it is accomplished" (Luke 12:50). Again and again He was tempted to turn aside from the path of costly obedience; in the wilderness, by the deadly machinations of the Evil One; at Caesarea Philippi, by Peter's misguided zeal; at Calvary, by the satiric taunts of His enemies. On the mount of transfiguration He faced once again the implications of His vocation. As He was praying, He was transfigured, and there appeared Moses and Elijah — the pre-eminent representatives of the law and the prophets — talking with Him. The subject of their discourse was His "exodus" which He must accomplish in Jerusalem (Luke 9: 31). Centuries before, a mighty exodus had been accomplished; now, another exodus is about to be. It accomplished, not a release from the bondage of Egypt, but a release from the bondage of sin, not by the death of the firstborn but by the death of Jesus, not for the children of Israel but for the children of men.

Peter and James and John saw the glory of Jesus as Moses and Elijah spoke with Him. Peter, ecstatically excited, cried out: " . . . let us make three booths, one for you and one for Moses and one for Elijah — not knowing what he said." And immediately "a cloud came and overshadowed them" (Luke 9:33, 34). It was no ordinary cloud: it was the cloud of the Shekinah, the cloud which, resting above the tent of meeting in the days of Moses, was the visible token of God's presence. " . . . they were afraid as they entered the cloud. And a voice came out of the cloud, saying, 'This is my Son, my Chosen; listen to him!' And when the voice had spoken, Jesus was found alone" (Luke 9:34-36).

No doubt Jesus might, like Enoch and Elijah, have been translated without the necessity of dying, but there was an "exodus" which He must accomplish in Jerusalem for the redemption of the world. So He came down from the mount, immediately to be confronted by a distracted father with an epileptic boy, a symbol of the world's desperate need.

In the garden of Gethsemane Jesus wrestled, once again, with the implications of obedience. "Father, if thou art willing," He prayed, "remove this cup from me; nevertheless, not my will, but thine, be done" (Luke 22:42). The agony was so intense that the sweat was like great drops of blood falling to the ground. And then He prayed again: "My Father, if this cannot pass unless I drink it, thy will be done" (Matthew 26:42). When the soldiers arrived to arrest Jesus, Peter attempted an impetuous defense. Jesus restrained him: "Put your sword into its sheath; shall I not drink the cup which the Father has given me?" (John 18:11).

Those who profess to be followers of Jesus are called upon to embrace a like vocation of service and sacrifice. The classic expression of this is to be found in St. Paul's letter to the Philippians where the Apostle writes:

> Have this mind among yourselves, which you have in Christ
> Jesus, who, though he was in the form of God, did not count
> equality with God a thing to be grasped, but emptied him-
> self, taking the form of a servant, being born in the likeness
> of men. And being found in human form he humbled him-
> self and became obedient unto death, even death on a cross.
> Therefore God has highly exalted him and bestowed on him
> the name which is above every name, that at the name of
> Jesus every knee should bow, in heaven and on earth and
> under the earth, and every tongue confess that Jesus Christ
> is Lord, to the glory of God the Father (Philippians 2:5-11).

The apostle speaks of Jesus's amazing self-abnegation: as
He humbled Himself unto death — even the ignominious
death of the cross — so we must seek to practice a like humility and a like self-denial.

When urged to adopt the balcony approach to life we
need to remember the example of the Son of Man who "came
not to be served but to serve, and to give his life as a ransom
for many" (Mark 10:45).

> Draw in the latchstring, lad, and close the door,
> Lest those who faint without from toil and pain
> Shall rob thee of thine own too meagre store.
> Such is the world's advice.
> But — there was One who flung it open wide —
> And He was crucified.

IV

There are two philosophies of life: there is the balcony
approach and the approach from the road. The one leads
to death in the midst of life and the other to life in the midst
of death. "For whoever would save his life," Jesus says, "will
lose it, and whoever loses his life for my sake will find it"
(Matthew 16:25). Paradoxically, it is only "as dying [that],
. . . behold, we live" (II Corinthians 6:9).

"If any man would come after me," Jesus says, "let him
deny himself, and take up his cross and follow me" (Matthew 16:24). If we would be disciples of the One who
pleased not Himself (Romans 15:3), we, too, must come
down from the balcony into the road.

Luther, in a moving passage, speaks of the subduing example of Jesus and the nature of his own personal resolution.

> When God in His sheer mercy and without any merit of mine has given me such unspeakable riches, shall I not then, freely, joyously, wholeheartedly, unprompted, do everything that I know to please Him? I will give myself as a sort of Christ to my neighbour as Christ gave Himself for me." [3]

For Studdert-Kennedy in like manner, there was only one possible response.

I bet my life

Upon one side in life's great war. I must.
I can't stand out. I must take sides. The man
Who is a neutral is this fight is not
A man. He's bulk and body without breath.
I want to live, live out, not wobble through
My life somehow, and then into the dark.
I must have God. This life's to dull without.
Too dull for ought but suicide.

I can't stand shivering on the bank. I plunge
Head first. [4]

---

[3] Quoted, R. H. Bainton, *Here I Stand: A Life of Martin Luther* (London: Hodder and Stoughton, 1951), p. 231.
[4] Quoted, J. A. Mackay, *op. cit.*, p. 48.

Chapter Nine

THE ART OF BEING KIND

Ella Wheeler Wilcox, the American humanist, was contemptuous of creeds and churches. She believed that the answer to the world's ills is to be found in something far less complex and confusing than doctrines and dogmas. She wrote:

> So many gods, so many creeds,
> So many paths that wind and wind,
> When just the art of being kind
> Is all this sad world needs. [1]

Her advice is deceptive in its very simplicity: "just the art of being kind." But how are men, who are naturally selfish, to learn the "art of being kind?"

Dr. Samuel Johnson was once asked: "Sir, do you not believe that man is naturally good?" to which he impatiently replied: "No more than a wolf!" [2] If man is naturally rapacious and predatory, selfish and self-seeking, how is he to learn the "art of being kind?" How are the teeth of the wolf to be drawn, and how is the beast to be tamed and trained? Is it sufficient to say, with Tennyson:

> More upward; working out the beast,
> And let the ape and tiger die?

[1] "The World's Need"
[2] James Boswell, *The Journal of a Tour to the Hebrides with Samuel Johnson* (London, 1955), p. 148.

I

It is a characteristic humanist delusion to affirm that advice and exhortation are sufficient to counteract and overcome human perversity, and to say that a man can reform himself by simply making good resolutions.

Thomas Carlyle, who was often critical of the Church, was once seated with his aged mother by the fireside at Ecclefechan. He was inveighing against the preachers of the day, as was his custom, when he suddenly concluded: "If I had to preach, I would go into the pulpit and say no more than this: 'All you people know what you ought to do; well, go and do it.'" His mother, a devout soul, continued knitting in silence, and then replied: "Aye, Tammas, and will ye tell them how?" [3]

There is, of course, all the difference in the world between knowing what is right, and doing it. Our problem is not ignorance but impotence. We know and approve the better, Ovid sadly confesses, and do the worse. We do not need finer ethical codes nor new moral systems — that is not our problem; what we need is the strength to do that which we know to be right. "To know," Cardinal Newman insists, "is one thing, to do is another; the two things are altogether distinct." [4]

Samuel Coleridge is a case in point. He was a hopeless slave to opium. His addiction was a mania. He knew that opium is a drug which enslaves and eventually destroys. He knew the imperative and immediate need for abstinence and amendment. He hired a man to watch him day and night, only to spend his time seeking to deceive the very man he was paying to watch him. He knew what was right, and yet, he was powerless to do it.

James Boswell relates a characteristic incident. He tells us that, on Sunday, November 28, 1762, he attended church.

[3] Quoted, J. S. Whale, *The Protestant Tradition* (New York: Cambridge University Press, 1955), p. 16.

[4] C. S. Dessain, *John Henry Newman* (New Jersey: Thomas Nelson & Sons, 1966), p. 69.

I went to St. James Church and heard service and a good sermon on "By what means shall a young man learn to order his ways," in which the advantages of early piety were well displayed. What a curious, inconsistent thing is the mind of man! In the midst of divine service I was laying plans for having women, and yet I had the most sincere feelings of religion. [5]

James Boswell, like many another, knew and approved the better, but did the worse.

II

What is the answer to the inveterate problem of human perversity? Is education the answer? Glory, science, knowledge, "and whatever other fine names we use," Newman reminded Sir Robert Peel, never healed a wounded heart, nor changed a sinful one. "You do not get rid of vice by human expedients; you can but use them according to circumstances, and in their place, as making the best of a bad matter. You must go to a higher source for the renovation of the heart and will. You do but play a sort of 'hunt the slipper' with the fault of our nature, till you go to Christianity." "People say to me," he continued, "that it is but a dream to suppose that Christianity should regain the organic power in human society which it once possessed. I cannot help that. I never said it could. I am not a politician; I am proposing no measures, but exposing a fallacy and resisting a pretence." [6]

Bertrand Russell acknowledges that we need, in our world today, the virtues of charity and compassion, of courage and hope, of kindness and love. He affirms:

> There are certain things that our age needs. . . . It needs compassion and a wish that mankind should be happy: it needs the desire for knowledge and the determination to eschew ancient myths; it needs, above all, courageous hope and the impulse of creativeness . . . the root of the matter

[5] Boswell's *London Journal 1762-1763* (London: Wm. Heinemann, 1952), p. 62. Quoted by permission.
[6] Dessain, *op. cit.*, pp. 69-70.

is a very simple and old fashioned thing, a thing so simple that I am almost ashamed to mention it for fear of the derisive smile with which wise cynics will greet my words. The thing I mean — please forgive me for mentioning it — is love, Christian love, or compassion. [7]

No one can quarrel with Bertrand Russell's moving diagnosis of our need, but what of his prescription? Is exhortation sufficient? Is it sufficient to say, with Ella Wheeler Wilcox, "just the art of being kind / Is all this sad world needs"?

The solution is not so simple. Within us all there are dark, demonic forces; there is, within us all, a "downward pull," a perversion of the will, a bias towards evil, a fatal flaw.

Augustine tells us, in a revealing passage of *The Confessions*, that as a boy he often prayed this prayer: "O God, give me chastity," only to add the words, "but not yet." He realized, years later, that his prayer was only a miserable self-deceit.

The humanist, however, is exceedingly reluctant to admit that the heart of man is not pure. He tends to close his eyes to the evidence of perversity in the life of man, to the fact that "we are betrayed by what is false within." But the humanist analysis is not only nauseating in its complacency; it is dangerously unrealistic. As T. E. Hulme once said, with mordant wit, "It is as if you pointed out to an old lady at a garden party that there was an escaped lion twenty yards away, and she was to reply, 'Oh yes,' and quietly take another cucumber sandwich." [8] But humanism will not do. Its analysis of human nature is as superficial as it is sentimental. We are corrupt and our wisdom is to confess it.

III

The Apostle Paul was brought up in the strictest tradition of the Jews. He sought to observe with punctilious care and

[7] *Impact of Science on Society* (New York: Columbia University Press, 1951), p. 59. Quoted by permission.

[8] Quoted, J. S. Whale, *Christian Doctrine* (New York: Cambridge University Press, 1941), p. 35.

scrupulous exactitude the ceremonial and ritual requirements of the law; he prided himself upon being a Pharisee of the Pharisees. Outwardly, his life was one of blameless rectitude. And yet, he was unhappily aware of inner failure and secret betrayal, of a conflict between the law of God in his mind and the law of sin in his members. Despite his achievements in righteousness, he was aware of the impure sin of covetousness. "I delight," he writes, "in the law of God, in my inmost self, but I see in my members another law at war with the law of my mind and making me captive to the law of sin which dwells in my members" (Romans 7:22, 23). The problem, he explains, was not infirmity of mind but weakness of will; an inability to do that which he knew to be right. "I can will what is right," he confesses, "but I cannot do it. For I do not do the good I want, but the evil I do not want is what I do" (Romans 7:18, 19). In his anguished unhappiness, he could only cry: "Wretched man that I am! Who will deliver me from this body of death?" (Romans 7: 24). The burden of sin, the perpetual conflict was, he said, insupportable; it was like being tied to the putrefying body of a corpse.

John Drinkwater speaks feelingly of our tragic inability, through moral impotence, to do that which we know to be right.

> Grant us the will to fashion as we feel,
> Grant us the strength to labor as we know,
> Grant us the purpose, ribbed and edged with steel,
>   To strike the blow.
> Knowledge we ask not. Knowledge thou has lent.
> But, Lord, the will: there lies our bitter need.
> Grant us to build above the deep intent
>   The deed, the deed.

It is through the grace and goodness of God that we are enabled "to build above the deep intent the deed." "But thanks be to God," Paul exultantly proclaims, "who gives us the victory through our Lord Jesus Christ" (I Corinthians 15:57).

IV

F. J. Foakes-Jackson boldly affirms, from a study of church history, that "the thought of Christ on the Cross has been more potent than anything else in arousing a compassion for suffering and indignation at injustice." [9] What this sad world needs, we believe, is not exhortation but evangelism, not good advice but good news, not the art of being kind but the grace of God in regeneration and renewal.

"I find," David Brainerd testifies, in the *Journal of his Life and Doings amongst the North American Indians,* "my Indians begin to put on the garments of holiness, and their common life begins to be sanctified even in a trifle when they are possessed by the doctrine of Christ, and Him crucified." "I never got away from Jesus, and Him crucified," he repeats, "and I found that when my people were gripped by this great evangelical doctrine of Christ, and Him crucified, I had no need to give them instructions about morality. I found that one followed as the sure and inevitable fruit of the other." [10]

"All treatises to promote holiness," Henry Venn affirms, "must be deplorably defective, unless the cross of Christ be laid as the foundation, constantly kept in view, and every duty enforced as having relation to the Redeemer."

A secular rationalist historian confirms the accuracy of this judgment: W. E. H. Lecky testifies,

> The doctrines the Methodist teacher taught, the theory of life he enforced, proved themselves capable of arousing in great masses of men an enthusiasm of piety which was hardly surpassed in the first days of Christianity, of eradicating inveterate vice, of fixing and directing impulsive and impetuous natures that were rapidly hastening towards the abyss. . . . [Methodism] planted a fervid and enduring religious sentiment in the midst of the most brutal and neglected portions of the population. [11]

[9] Cambridge Theological Essays (New York: Macmillan, 1905), p. 512f.
[10] Quoted, J. H. Jowett, *Apostolic Optimism* (London: Hodder and Stoughton, 1902), p. 84.
[11] *A History of England in the Eighteenth Century* (London: Longmans, Green & Company, 1892), Volume III, pp. 100-1.

John Wesley had a ready explanation for these things: they were, he believed, an inevitable concomitant of the earnest and faithful preaching of the gospel.

> I have seen (as far as a thing of this kind can be seen) very many persons changed in a moment from the spirit of fear, horror, despair, to the spirit of love, joy and peace; and from sinful desire, till then reigning over them, to a pure desire of doing the will of God. . . I will show you him that was a lion till then, and is now a lamb; him that was a drunkard, and is now exemplarily sober; the whoremonger that was, who now abhors the very "garment spotted by the flesh." These are my living arguments . . . [12]

The one thing you cannot refute, it has been said, is the testimony of a life. You can refute an argument but you cannot successfully refute a life.

Christianity's indictment of human nature may be radical but it is also realistic. What Christianity affirms is that, as is the root, so is the fruit; that as a good tree can bring forth nothing but good fruit, so a bad tree can bring forth nothing but bad fruit (Matthew 7:17). Because of the corruption of our nature it is only the man who is rooted and grounded in Christ who can bring forth fruit unto holiness. " . . . if any one is in Christ," the apostle triumphantly proclaims, "he is a new creation; the old has passed away, behold, the new has come" (II Corinthians 5:17).

"Just the art of being kind" sounds deceptively simple, but it is not within our power; what is required, for this achievement, is a miracle of grace: the presence and power of the One who says, "Behold, I make all things new" (Revelation 21:5).

---

[12] Quoted, V. H. H. Green, *John Wesley* (London: Nelson, 1964), p. 75.

Chapter Ten

REDEEMING THE TIME

A distinguished explorer recently attempted a forced march through the jungles of the Upper Amazon in company with a party of natives. They made unusually good progress for the first two days but, on the third, when it was time to start, the explorer found that his natives were sitting on their haunches, looking very solemn, and making no preparations to leave. "They are waiting," the Chief explained, "they cannot go further until their souls have caught up with their bodies."

I

Our Western civilization is tyrannized by the clock. Lewis Mumford regards the clock and not the machine as the characteristic symbol of our technological age. "It marks," he says, "a perfection towards which other machines aspire." The abolition of the clock would, he suggests, precipitate the speedy disruption and eventual collapse of our society. "The modern industrial regime could do without coal and iron and steam easier than it could do without the clock." [1]

From our earliest years we find ourselves dominated by the clock. As children, we become accustomed to the authoritarian words: "Time to go to bed," "Time to get up." As men, we endure the humiliating drudgery of being required to "clock in." And yet, despite the reiterated command to

[1] *Technics and Civilization* (New York: Harcourt, Brace & Co., 1934), pp. 14-17. Quoted by permission.

be "on time" and "not to waste time," we find ourselves complaining that we "never have time."

It is not only industry which is dominated by the clock, it is also the organic functions of life. We are required to eat, not when we feel hungry, but when prompted by the clock; we are required to sleep, not when we feel tired, but when sanctioned by the clock.

II

The life of man in society is marked by constant unrest, by what we might describe as time panic.

Emil Brunner attributes this to the loss of a sense of eternity. Man, he suggests, has no time, is always short of time, because he has no other horizon than the temporal. He has a compulsive desire to compress into the brief compass of life every conceivable possibility, every human experience. Time, we say, waits for no man, time marches on. Natural man is haunted by the fear of the closed door. He is always looking at his watch, he is always demanding the exact radio time, he is time crazy, and yet, he protests that he never has time. [2]

Eastern man, by contrast, always has time. In the East, time is an illusion. It has no reality. Eternity alone is real. The temporal world is only appearance.

Time, therefore, is nothing. It is worthless, unreal. That is why the Eastern man is in no hurry. He always has time.

III

The natural man has an instinctive awareness of the fleeting impermanence of time. He is morbidly conscious of the inevitability of time, of the ineluctable passage of time. That is why he eagerly snatches at each moment of time, that is why he seeks to extract from time everything possible. Robert Herrick, in a poem addressed "To the Virgins," argues the wisdom of making "much of time":

[2] *Christianity and Civilization* (New York: Scribner's, 1948), Volume 1, p. 48.

Gather ye rosebuds while ye may,
Old Time is still a-flying,
And this same flower that smiles today
Tomorrow will be dying.

The glorious lamp of Heaven, the sun,
The higher he's a getting;
The sooner will his race be run,
And nearer he's to setting.

That age is best, which is the first,
When youth and blood are warmer;
But being spent, the worse, and worst
Times, still succeed the former.

Then be not coy, but use your time;
And while ye may, go marry:
For having lost but once your prime,
You may for ever tarry.

For the Christian man, the significance of time is not to be found in the frantic pursuit of sensual pleasure but in the experience of the reality of God.

With the Persian poet the natural man seeks to obliterate from his consciousness an awareness of time's remorseless march by an intense preoccupation with the present.

Ah, fill the Cup — What boots it to repeat
How Time is slipping underneath our Feet:
Unborn Tomorrow, and dead Yesterday,
Why fret about them if Today is sweet!

". . . the wicked," the prophet derisively observes, "are like the tossing sea; for it cannot rest, and its waters toss up mire and dirt" (Isaiah 57:20). Speaking of his unregenerate days, Augustine describes the manner in which he sought to evade the disturbing reality of God: "I sought to lose myself in a multiplicity of things," he says.

The Christian man is neither anxiously preoccupied with time nor is he indifferent to it. He is neither tyrannized by time nor oblivious of it. He takes time seriously. He seeks to make a constructive and creative use of time. He knows that time is important. Time is a trust.

We are immersed in the temporal time process. We are caught up in the remorseless passage of time. Time flies. That is why we are to buy up the time. We are to adopt an attitude neither of panicked frenzy nor of disinterested aloofness. We are to redeem the time (Ephesians 5:16). We are to make time the servant of eternity.

IV

It is not time itself which is important; it is, of course, what happens *in* time which is the important thing. We recognize this when we speak of special times, times of more than usual significance. Churchill, in the days of crisis and catastrophe after the fall of France, testified: "I felt as if I was walking with destiny, and that all my past life had been but a preparation for this hour and this time." The invasion of Normandy was called D-Day: it was the day of decisive and determinative significance in relation to the future progress of the war; in a far more profound sense Jesus spoke of His suffering and death as His "hour."

In common parlance we speak of "the hour of destiny," "the eleventh hour," "zero hour." The Rumanian novelist, C. Virgil Gheorghiu, entitled a recent novel, *The Twenty-fifth Hour.* A new hybrid monstrosity, he says, is in the process of supplanting man from the face of the earth. These aborted creatures, he explains,

> do not live in the jungle or the forests, but in offices. Yet they are more ferocious than the beasts of the jungle. They are the bastard breed of man and machine — a degenerate breed, but today the most powerful on earth. Their faces are the faces of men, and outwardly they are indistinguishable from human beings. But soon enough it becomes obvious that they don't behave like human beings. They behave exactly like machines. They have chronometers in place of hearts . . . . They are citizens . . . a strange mongrel type. They have gone forth and multiplied to the ends of the earth. [3]

[3] (London: William Heinemann, 1950), p. VIII. Quoted by permission.

Why is this the Twenty-fifth Hour? It is the hour past mid-night, the hour when all hope is gone. Gabriel Marcel de-scribes this disturbing novel as "the *De Profundis* of an ago-nized humanity." [4]

V

The Christian faith affirms that each moment of temporal time can become a moment of eternal significance. Francis Thompson speaks of

> . . . what Time in mists confounds;
> Yet ever and anon a triumph sounds
> From the hid battlements of Eternity.

God speaks in the midst of time. To man, caught up in life's fever and fret, God speaks, saying: "Be still, and know that I am God" (Psalm 46:10).

The Greeks used two different words for our one word "time": *kronos* and *kairos. Kronos* means duration, meas-ured time; *kairos,* the appointed time, the appropriate time, the time of fulfillment. True life, rightly understood, is more than an aggregation of happenings; true life is more than measured time. It is life filled with significance, it is decision in the midst of duration, it is opportunity and occasion find-ing expression in action and response. Any moment in his-torical time can be, in the inscrutable providence of God, a day of crisis and decision; any date on the calendar can become a day of unique fulfillment.

There are, for all of us, dates on the almanac which are forever charged with more than usual significance, days and times hallowed by sacred associations and tender memories. For some it is the ecstatic experience of marriage or the birth of a child.

God, too, has "his times *(kronoi)* and seasons *(kairoi)*" (Acts 1:7; Titus 1:2, 3). Thus, " . . . when the time had fully come, God sent forth his Son, born of woman, born under the law, to redeem those who were under the law, so that we might receive adoption as sons" (Galatians 4:4, 5).

[4] *Ibid.,* Preface in the French edition, p. xi.

> Then came, at a predetermined moment, a moment in time and of time,
> A moment not out of time, but in time, in what we call history: transecting, bisecting the world of time, a moment in time but not like a moment of time,
> A moment in time but time was made through that moment: for without the meaning there is no time, and that moment of time gave the meaning. [5]

The poet, of course, is referring to the coming of Christ, and its significance for the world. As a consequence, the Apostle is able to say: "Behold, now is the acceptable time (*kairos*), behold, now is the day of salvation" (II Corinthians 6:2). Every moment is now, for every man, a day of opportunity, a time of grace; for every man *kronos* time is *kairos* time.

Because the Jews were unable to discern the signs of the times (Matthew 16:3), they remained obdurately blind to the saving significance of Jesus. Towards the end of His ministry, Jesus sorrowfully wept over Jerusalem, saying:

> Would that even today you knew the things that make for peace! But now they are hid from your eyes. For the days shall come upon you, when your enemies will cast up a bank about you and surround you, and hem you in on every side, and dash you to the ground, you and your children within you, and they will not leave one stone upon another in you; because you did not know the time of your visitation" (Luke 19:41-44).

Kronos time is now *kairos* time. "O that today you would hearken to his voice!" the Psalmist cries (Psalm 95:7). Unhappily, there are many who do not hear. There are many of whom it must be said that "seeing they do not see, and hearing they do not hear, nor do they understand" (Matthew 13:13). For the man whose eyes have been opened, and whose ears have been unstopped, however, life is irradiated with light, and time is filled with eternity.

Because the days are evil, the Christian man must earnest-

[5] T. S. Eliot *The Rock: A Pageant Play* (London: Faber and Faber, 1934), p. 50. Quoted by permission.

ly seek to understand what the will of the Lord is (Ephesians 5:15-17). "So . . . live," writes the Apostle Peter, "for the rest of the time in the flesh no longer by human passions but by the will of God. Let the time that is past," he warns, "suffice for doing what the Gentiles like to do, living in licentiousness, passions, drunkenness, revels, carousing, and lawless idolatry" (I Peter 4:2, 3).

The time is short: we are to avoid a life of foolish dissipation and to live responsibly, because the day is coming when there will be time *(kronos)* no longer (Revelation 10: 6).

> Take care, brethren, lest there be in any of you an evil, unbelieving heart, leading you to fall away from the living God. But exhort one another every day, as long as it is called "today," that none of you may be hardened by the deceitfulness of sin (Hebrews 3:12, 13).

PART II

Chapter Eleven

FROM HOLLYWOOD TO HEAVEN

In these days of semantic confusion the word love, it has been said, can mean anything from Hollywood to Heaven.

What do we mean when we say, in summary fashion, that God is love? (I John 4:8). Our very familiarity with this affirmation tends to dull its startling originality. We might say that "John has an affectionate nature"; we might say that "John is loving"; but we would never say that "John is love." And yet, in relation to God, we say, not that He is loving, but that He is love. In speaking of God, we insist that love is more than an attribute, we insist that love belongs to His essence: that, in His very self, He is love.

At this point we may illustrate what we mean by the bold declaration that God is love, by employing, for illustrative purposes, three analogies: the analogy of a man's love for his friends; the analogy of a man's love for his wife; and the analogy of a man's love for his son.

I

First, the analogy of a man's love for his friends.

Alexander Russell, a former student of Trinity College, Glenalmond, Scotland, was sent, during the days of *World War I*, to his regiment in India. He sailed on the *S. S. Birkenhead*. In the tropics the ship was torpedoed and sank. Russell found himself in charge of a lifeboat crowded to capacity with men, women, and children. Crouched near him, on the gunwale, there was a young mother, nursing her infant baby.

Suddenly, she saw her husband struggling helplessly in the water, and hysterically she cried for someone to save him. Without hesitation, Alexander Russell dived overboard, rescued the man, gave him his place on the boat, then swam away to meet certain death in the shark infested waters. Concerning such a deed of splendid and selfless heroism we are moved to say: "Greater love hath no man than this, that a man lay down his life for his friends" (John 15:13).

"Peradventure," writes the Apostle Paul, "for a good man some would even dare to die." That is certainly true. Indeed, we might hope that, if we found ourselves in circumstances similar to those in which Alexander Russell found himself, we would make a like response. But the question is whether we would make the same response for a racist or a rapist, a rogue or a scoundrel. Paul points out: ". . . for a good man some would even dare to die, but God" — and this is the decisive difference — "commendeth his love toward us, in that, while we were yet sinners, Christ died for us" (Romans 5:7, 8, KJV).

We think of a man's love for his friends, and we rightly acknowledge that such love is a noble and splendid thing, a sublime and selfless thing; and then we remember that Jesus laid down his life, not for His friends, but His enemies, and that, on the cross, He prayed for those who mocked and derided Him.

We rightly commemorate the nobility of human love when it is exemplified in heroic self-sacrifice; but, on the cross, we see exemplified a love which, by its very inclusiveness, is qualitatively different, a love which, in the last analysis, is not human, but divine. "To have died for valuable men," C. S. Lewis rightly observes, "would have been not divine but merely heroic; but God died for sinners." [1] Luther makes the same point. Human love, he observes, is always a broken arc: it stops short somewhere, as we find we cannot love those who are ugly or evil or who do not love us. But God's love is a perfect circle, for He loves the evil and the good.

[1] Quoted, Sherwood E. Wirt, *The Social Conscience of the Evangelical* (New York: Harper & Row, 1968), p. 72.

II

Secondly, the analogy of a man's love for his wife.

The prophet Hosea was commanded by God to marry a woman of loose morals. In obedience to the divine command he married Gomer, a woman of the streets. Gomer bore three children and Hosea was happy in the love of his wife and the joy of his family. And then, for some strange and inscrutable reason, the appeal of her old life reasserted itself, and she abandoned her children and deserted her husband and left their home, resuming her former life of sordid degradation as a woman of the streets. For Hosea, it was a time of private hurt and public humiliation. There came a time, however, when her beauty departed, Gomer was no longer desirable. Abandoned and alone, destitute and diseased, she found herself exposed for sale in the market square as a common slave. Then the word of the Lord came to Hosea commanding him to purchase his wife again. So he bought her for fifteen pieces of silver. In the privacy and seclusion of their home, he sought to re-awaken her love.

Through this harrowing domestic tragedy Hosea learned something of what man's base ingratitude means to God. "When Israel was a child, I loved him," God says, "and out of Egypt I called my son." Israel's response to God's love, however, was not filial gratitude but infidelity and ingratitude: "The more I called them," God accuses, "the more they went from me; they kept sacrificing to the Baals, and burning incense to idols" (Hosea 11:1, 2). Hosea learned something of the sorrow in the heart of God: the anguish of spurned and rejected love. "I led them," God confides, "with cords of compassion, with the bands of love, . . . " (Hosea 11: 4).

We think of a man's love for his wife, and we rightly say that married love is a beautiful, holy thing; but, in this life, marital love, even at its best, is a frail and fragile thing, easily spoiled and shattered by cruelty and drunkenness and selfishness and sin. God's love, by contrast, is not fleeting and ephemeral; it is enduring and eternal. "I have loved you,"

God testifies, "with an everlasting love; therefore I have continued my faithfulness to you" (Jeremiah 31:3).

III

Thirdly, the analogy of a man's love for his son.
Martin Jarrett-Kerr has written an arresting modern adaptation of the parable of the prodigal son:

> Once upon a time there was a young man who had come of age and determined to go out and earn his own living. He went to his Father and asked him for the allowance that was due to him, and set forth. He traveled a long way in his exploration and after many adventures fell into bad company. Gradually all his allowance was used up, and still he could not shake himself free from the enticements. At last he was penniless, and was driven to take service under a prominent farmer there, who put him to look after the pigs; and not only look after them, but even to share their diet. In this plight he suddenly woke up: even the servants at home, he thought, are better off than I. Is it too late now for me to go back? Surely not. I will arise and go to my Father, and say to him: Father, I have sinned against heaven and in your sight, and I am no more worthy to be called a son of yours; but at least make me one of your servants.
>
> So he traveled back the long journey home. It was winter, and as he came near the house he could see lights in the distance, and coming closer still, he heard music and voices from inside. He half wondered whether, by some coincidence, his Father might happen to be looking out through a window and see him coming and run out to meet him. But no one came. He made his way through the snow, and at last reached the front door. He knocked, but there was no answer. Remembering the noise that was going on inside, he knocked again, and louder. After a long wait and more knocking, he heard the bolts being drawn, and at last the door was opened.
>
> His Father stood in the entrance, peering out into the night. "Father," he cried, "It's me! Your son. I've made an awful mess of things, I'm afraid. I know it's all my fault, but honestly I will try. Will you take me back — just as one of your servants. . . ?" His Father looked at him strangely.

"My son? I only have one son, and he is inside with me."
"But, Father," said the boy, "I'm your other boy — your
second son." His Father shook his head slowly. "I have no
second son," he said, and shut the door. And as the boy
turned and walked away slowly into the snow, he could
hear behind him the noise of music and voices. [2]

What a contrast there is between this all-too-human father
who, in implacable anger, unrelenting and unforgiving, refused to hear the cry of his penitent son, and the father of
whom we read in the gospel, who was eagerly watching and
waiting for his son, who, when his son was yet a great way
off, saw him, and ran, and had compassion, and fell on his
neck, and kissed him, and said: "Bring quickly the best robe,
and put it on him; and put a ring on his hand, and shoes on
his feet; and bring the fatted calf and kill it, and let us eat
and make merry; for this my son was dead, and is alive again;
he was lost, and is found" (Luke 15:22-24).

We think of a man's love for his son, and we rightly celebrate such love as a tender, precious thing; but we remember
that even a father or a mother's love can change from patient
forbearance to angry hostility, from acceptance to rejection.
The prophet Isaiah asks the pointed question: "Can a woman forget her sucking child, that she should have no compassion on the son of her womb?" God sadly replies: "Even
these may forget, yet I will not forget you" (Isaiah 49:15).

William Cowper points the contrast between the fragility
of familial love and the indestructibility of God's love:

> Can a woman's tender care
> Cease towards the child she bare?
> Yes, she may forgetful be,
> Yet will I remember thee.

Cowper lyrically pictures God as saying:

> Mine is an unchanging love,
> Higher than the heights above,
> Deeper than the depths beneath,
> Free and faithful, strong as death.

[2] *Our Trespasses* (London: S.C.M. Press, 1948), pp. 69-70.

IV

Finally, analogies fail. If we want to know what God's love is like, then we look at a naked Man nailed to a cross, and we hear the Apostle John say: "In this is love, not that we loved God but that he loved us and sent his Son to be the expiation for our sins" (I John 4:10).

God is love, and the supreme demonstration of this subduing fact is to be found in the death of the Son of God. "For God so loved the world that he gave his only Son, that whoever believes in him should not perish but have eternal life" (John 3:16).

It is not surprising that the writers of the New Testament were hard put to it to find a word which might fittingly and worthily describe love of this kind and of this quality. The common Greek word for love, *eros*, means love for the lovely; the early Christians needed a less limited word, a qualitatively different word, a word indicative of the transvaluation of values effected by the life and death of Jesus. They therefore appropriated, as a more adequate word, the word *agape*.

The fundamental differences may be indicated by a series of contrasts: Whereas *eros* is concerned with getting, *agape* is concerned with giving; whereas *eros* is selfish and possessive, *agape* is self-giving; whereas *eros* is aroused by the worthiness of the object loved, *agape* is neither aroused nor allayed by the worthiness or the unworthiness of the object loved; whereas *eros* is the reward of merit and desert, *agape* is free, unmerited and undeserved. Whereas, says G. B. Caird simply, *eros* is all take; *agape* is all give. [3]

V

Soren Kierkegaard testifies to the power of such love to evoke love: "I am," he humbly confesses,

> a poor wretch whom God took charge of, and for whom He had done so indescribably much more than I ever expected, oh, so indescribably much more that I only long for the peace of eternity in order to do nothing but thank Him. As

[3] *The Truth of the Gospel* (London: University Press, 1950), p. 112.

a man, personally I am, in a more than general sense, a sinner who has been far along the road to perdition — a sinner who nevertheless believes that all his sins are forgiven him for Christ's sake, even though he must bear the result of punishment; a sinner who longs for eternity in order to thank Him and His love. [4]

The Apostle John gives a like testimony: "We love, because he first loved us" (I John 4:19).

Christians, down the ages, have been moved to say, with Isaac Watts:

> When I survey the wondrous Cross
> On which the Prince of glory died,
> My richest gain I count but loss,
> And pour contempt on all my pride.
>
> Forbid it, Lord, that I should boast,
> Save in the Cross of Christ, my God:
> All the vain things that charm me most,
> I sacrifice them to His Blood.
>
> See, from His head, His hands, His feet,
> Sorrow and love flow mingled down:
> Did e'er such love and sorrow meet,
> Or thorns compose so rich a crown?
>
> Were the whole realm of nature mine,
> That were an offering far too small;
> Love so amazing, so divine,
> Demands my soul, my life, my all.

[4] *The Journals of Soren Kierkegaard,* edited and translated by Alexander Dru (London: Oxford University Press, 1938), p. 257.

Chapter Twelve

BREAKING DOWN THE DIVIDING WALL

A few months before his assassination, President Kennedy, speaking of the struggle for racial justice, made this comment:

> We are confronted primarily with a moral issue. It is as old as the Scriptures and as clear as the American Constitution. The heart of the question is whether all Americans are to be afforded equal rights and equal opportunities. Those who do nothing are inviting shame and violence. Those who act boldly are recognizing right as well as reality. [1]

The churches, unfortunately, have tended to follow rather than to lead in this matter. The churches, Martin Luther King bluntly charges, "have all too often been more cautious than courageous, and have remained silent behind the anesthetizing security of stained-glass windows." [2]

I

Is there, we need to ask, theological justification for a stance on those things that bitterly divide us: race and class and sex? What is the significance of the apostle's ringing declaration that "there is neither Jew nor Greek, there is neither slave nor free, there is neither male nor female; for you are all one in Christ Jesus"? (Galatians 3:28).

An orthodox male Jew, in his daily morning prayer, thanked God that he had not been born a Gentile, a slave,

---

[1] Quoted, Martin Luther King, Jr., *Why We Can't Wait* (New York: The New American Library, 1964), p. 32. Quoted by permission.
[2] *Op. cit.*, p. 90.

or a woman. (A Jewish woman, by contrast, dolefully thanked God that she was as God had made her!) Prior to his conversion Paul, as a devout and dedicated Jew, dutifully prayed this prayer. After his conversion, he began to see things in a new way and in a different light, from a new perspective and a different point of view. He boldly took this traditional prayer of Judaism and he reversed it. Whereas he had formerly thanked God that he had not been born a Gentile, a slave, or a woman, he now thanked God that, in Christ, "there is neither Jew nor Greek, there is neither slave nor free, there is neither male nor female."

This is what conversion meant for Paul; a transvaluation, a change of outlook, a reorientation of heart and mind, a transformation that was as radical as it was revolutionary. And one immediate consequence was, that those he had formerly abhorred he now accepted.

II

In the first place, there is neither Jew nor Greek.

To a religious Jew, a Gentile was despised as one ignorant of the law. The Gentiles, it was said, had been created as fuel for the fires of hell. A Jewish woman was forbidden to render help to a Gentile mother in her hour of trial lest she thereby incur responsibility for helping to bring another Gentile into the world. A Jewish boy, having married a Gentile girl, was cut off as one dead and the funeral office was read for him. To go into a Gentile home was to risk ritual contamination and exclusion from the services of the temple. (Thus, the Jewish leaders, at the time of the trial of Jesus, refused to enter the house of Pontius Pilate, the Roman Governor, lest they thereby be ceremonially defiled and precluded from eating the Passover feast.)

The Samaritans were, of all races, objects of special execration. They were despised as half breeds and detested as apostates. The very word Samaritan became a term of contemptuous scorn in the vocabulary of a Jew. The deepest insult that could be hurled at Jesus was to accuse Him of being a Samaritan and having a devil (John 8:48). By a process of extension, to call a man a Samaritan was in effect to call him a mongrel or a dog.

The reaction of the Samaritan woman, at the well of Sychar, when Jesus first spoke to her (she, a woman!), and then asked her for a drink (she, a Samaritan!), was one of incredulous astonishment. "How is it that you, a Jew, ask a drink of me, a woman of Samaria?" The writer of the gospel narrative adds, by way of explanation, "for Jews have no dealings with the Samaritans" (John 4:9).

How radical and revolutionary was the change effected in traditional attitudes by the example of Jesus! Before the time of Christ, to call a man a Samaritan was an outrageous insult; since the time of Christ, it has been a generous compliment. If we ask how it was that a term of contempt was converted into a title of honor, the answer is a simple one: it was changed by Jesus. He talked to a woman of Samaria by a well, and He told a story about a robber infested road, a bleeding victim, a callous priest, an indifferent Levite, and a despised Samaritan. W. E. Sangster, in a colorful metaphor, says that Jesus picked the word Samaritan out of the gutter and washed it clean. He took that term from the vocabulary of the brothel and made it adjectival with the saints. [3]

Jesus showed, by His words and deeds, that He did not share the inherited attitudes and the irrational prejudices of His countrymen. Salvation, Jesus acknowledges, is of the Jews (John 4:22); they are the ones through whom the whole world is to be blessed. Simeon, greeting the infant Christ, acknowledged that He was to be a light to the Gentiles as well as the glory of God's people, Israel (Luke 2:32). "Woman, believe me," Jesus tells the Samaritan woman, "the hour is coming when neither on this mountain nor in Jerusalem will you worship the Father. . . . But the hour is coming," He continues, "and now is, when the true worshipers will worship the Father in spirit and in truth, for such the Father seeks to worship him" (John 4:21-23).

[3] *Westminster Sermons* (Tennessee: Abingdon Press, 1961), Volume II, p. 40.

In Christ there is no place for racial exclusiveness. Segregation is a contradiction and denial of the Gospel, for, in Christ, there is neither Jew nor Greek.

"But now in Christ Jesus," the apostle tells the Asian Christians in Ephesus,

> you who once were far off have been brought near in the blood of Christ. For he is our peace, who has made us both one, and has broken down the dividing wall of hostility, by abolishing in his flesh the law of commandments and ordinances, that he might create in himself one new man in place of the two, so making peace, and might reconcile us both to God in one body through the cross, thereby bringing the hostility to an end (Ephesians 2:13-16).

III

Secondly, there is neither slave nor free.

In the eyes of the law a man who was a slave was a living tool. A master, in relation to his slaves, had the power of life and death. It was a relationship which opened the door wide to callous inhumanity.

In the city of Rome, one quarter of the population were slaves. The constant fear of a slave uprising led to panic measures of appalling ferocity. The slightest breach of good behavior invited savage punishment. Every slave was branded. The punishment for insubordination was perpetual banishment to the mines; the sentence for escape or revolt was lingering death by crucifixion.

The relationship was degrading to both parties. Juvenal tells of the mistress who would beat her maidservant at her whim; of the master who delighted in the sound of a cruel flogging, "deeming it sweeter than any siren's song." If the relationship incited to sadism on the one hand it incited to corruption on the other, the slave revenging himself on his master by pandering to his vice.

This vicious relationship was revolutionized when Jesus invited, among others, those who were (in the Pauline phrase) despised as "the refuse of the world, and the offscouring of all things" (I Corinthians 4:13).

After the conversion of the runaway slave Onesimus, Paul sent him back to his Christian master, Philemon, "no longer as a slave but more than a slave, as a beloved brother, . . . " (Philemon 16). Onesimus, Paul pointedly reminds Philemon, is, as a consequence of his conversion, no longer a chattel but a Christian, no longer a bondservant but a brother.

The Christian community is a universal brotherhood, and it is not the exclusive preserve of the privileged few; on the contrary, it is open to all men irrespective of class. Indeed, if there is a bias, it is the other way:

> For consider your call, brethren; not many of you were wise according to worldly standards, not many were powerful, not many were of noble birth; but God chose what is foolish in the world to shame the wise, God chose what is weak in the world to shame the strong, God chose what is low and despised in the world, even things that are not, to bring to nothing things that are, so that no human being might boast in the presence of God (I Corinthians 1:26-29).

In Christ the differences of class, like the differences of race, have no ultimate significance; in Christ, there is, Paul reiterates, neither slave nor free.

IV

Thirdly, there is neither male nor female.

In the ancient world the position of women was one of social inferiority. Demosthenes cynically observes:

> We have courtesans for the sake of pleasure; we have concubines for the sake of daily cohabitation; we have wives for the purpose of having children legitimately, and of having a faithful guardian for all our household affairs.

Jesus revolutionized the status of women. He treated women with understanding and respect. They accompanied Him on His travels, without a breath of scandal, ministering to Him of their substance. They stood by Him in His agony. They were early at the tomb and the first to see Him on the day of resurrection.

What we find, within the Christian community, is equality

of status with difference of function. In the economy of God, in the affairs of this life, each sex has its special role to fulfill and its proper function; in the life of faith, in the realm of the spirit, we are all partakers of the same grace and of the same hope.

The differences of sex have no ultimate significance, they are a matter of temporary dispensation; in the world to come, Jesus points out, they neither marry nor are given in marriage (Matthew 22:30).

V

The unknown author of the Epistle to Diognetus celebrates the consequence of the coming of Christianity into the world. Within the Christian community the accidental differences of race and class and sex are not, of course, obliterated, but they are transcended and overcome. In Christ, a new unity is created, a unity derived not from birth but belief. "For the first time in human history," John MacMurray observes, "a human society was constructed by men on a basis which was not a basis of blood and soil; which did not rest upon organic impulse, but was the fruit of a religious belief in the spiritual brotherhood of man." "For the distinction between Christians, and other men," the anonymous author to Diognetus explains,

> is neither in country nor language nor customs. For they do not dwell in cities in some place of their own, nor do they use any strange variety of dialect, nor practice an extraordinary kind of life. This teaching of theirs has not been discovered by the intellect or thought of busy men, nor are they the advocates of any human doctrine as some men are. Yet while living in Greek and barbarian cities, according as each obtained his lot, and following the local customs, both in clothing and food and in the rest of life, they show forth the wonderful and confessedly strange character of the constitution of their own citizenship. They dwell in their own fatherlands, but as if sojourners in them; they share all things as citizens, and suffer all things as strangers. . . To put it shortly, what the soul is in the body the Christians are in the world.

> . . . The flesh hates the soul, and wages war upon it,
> though it has suffered no evil, because it is prevented from
> gratifying its pleasures, and the world hates the Christians
> though it has suffered no evil, because they are opposed to
> its pleasures. The soul loves the flesh which hates it and
> the limbs, and Christians love those that hate them. The
> soul has been shut up in the body, but itself sustains the
> body; and Christians are confined in the world as in a
> prison, but themselves sustain the world. The soul dwells
> immortal in a mortal tabernacle, and Christians sojourn
> among corruptible things, waiting for the incorruptibility
> which is in heaven. The soul when evil treated in food and
> drink becomes better, and Christians, when buffeted, day
> by day increase more. God has appointed them to so great
> a post and it is not right for them to decline it.

Through the life and death and resurrection of Jesus a new
society, a new community, a new commonwealth has been
inaugurated and established. Within this society the differences of race and class and sex are no longer divisive and
destructive; on the contrary, within this society, men and
women from every nation and tribe and tongue and people
find their unity in a new and creative relationship. "Here,"
the apostle joyfully proclaims, "there cannot be Greek and
Jew, circumcised and uncircumcised, barbarian, Scythian,
slave, free man, but Christ is all, and in all" (Colossians 3:
11).

Chapter Thirteen

BLOWIN' IN THE WIND

A note of sad and wistful longing pervades Bob Dylan's haunting folk song, "Blowin' in the Wind."

The theme of this song is man's inhumanity to man. When will there be an end, he plaintively asks, to the intractable problems of human selfishness and sin? When will there be an end to the bitter indignity of racial segregation, to the senseless futility of war and to the callous oppression of the weak? To each question he can only reply enigmatically that the answer is "blowin' in the wind."

I

And yet, in spite of the pervasive pessimism of Bob Dylan's sad poem, the folk singer was right: The answer *is* blowing in the wind: not, of course, in that wind which is an expression of the physical forces of nature, but in that wind which is a manifestation of God's Spirit, that rushing mighty wind which on the day of Pentecost descended upon the apostles, so that they were all filled with the Holy Spirit (Acts 2:2-4).

The wind, in the pages of the Bible, is frequently a metaphor for the Spirit of God: indeed, the very word *ruach* means not only "Spirit" but also "breath" and "wind."

The significance of this may be illustrated by reference to the experience of the prophet Ezekiel:

> The hand of the Lord was upon me, and he brought me out by the Spirit of the Lord, and set me down in the midst of the valley; it was full of bones. And he led me round

among them; and behold, there were very many upon the valley; and lo, they were very dry. And he said to me, "Son of man, can these bones live?" And I answered, "O Lord God, thou knowest." Again he said to me, "Prophesy to these bones, and say to them, O dry bones, hear the word of the Lord. Thus says the Lord God to these bones: Behold, I will cause breath to enter you, and you shall live. And I will lay sinews upon you, and will cause flesh to come upon you, and cover you with skin, and put breath in you, and you shall live; and you shall know that I am the Lord."

So I prophesied as I was commanded; and as I prophesied, there was a noise, and behold, a rattling; and the bones came together, bone to its bone. And as I looked, there were sinews on them, and flesh had come upon them, and skin had covered them; but there was no breath in them. Then he said to me, "Prophesy to the breath, prophesy, son of man, and say to the breath, Thus says the Lord God: Come from the four winds, O breath, and breathe upon these slain, that they may live." So I prophesied as he commanded me, and the breath came into them, and they lived, and stood upon their feet, an exceedingly great host (Ezekiel 37:1-10).

Can dead men live? Can dry bones be clothed with sinews and with flesh? Can men who are spiritually dead, dead in trespasses and sins (Ephesians 2:1), be raised to newness of life? To these questions there is no answer known to man. If the question is asked: "Can these bones live?" we can only reply, with the prophet Ezekiel: "O Lord God, thou knowest."

None but God has the power to kill and make alive (Deuteronomy 32:39); none but God has the power to say: "Come from the four winds, O breath, and breathe upon these slain, that they may live"; none but God can perform the miracle of regeneration and revivification.

Jesus had to remind Nicodemus of this humbling and disconcerting fact. "Truly, truly, I say to you, unless one is born anew, he cannot see the kingdom of God." Nicodemus was deeply perplexed: "How can a man be born when he is old? Can he enter a second time into his mother's womb and be born?" How can a man, he inquires, repeat the process of physical birth? Jesus replies that just as entry into this world is by the process of physical birth, so entry into the kingdom of God is conditional upon the experience of spiritual birth. Jesus points out that the prerequisite of spiritual understanding is spiritual rebirth.

> Truly, truly, I say to you, unless one is born of water and the Spirit, he cannot enter the kingdom of God. That which is born of the flesh is flesh and that which is born of the Spirit is spirit. Do not marvel that I said to you, "You must be born anew." The wind blows where it wills, and you hear the sound of it, but you do not know whence it comes or whither it goes; so it is with everyone who is born of the Spirit (John 3:5-8).

We do not know the origin nor the destination of the wind, nevertheless, Jesus explains, we see and hear its effects: the work of the Spirit in the life of a man is likewise mysterious and inscrutable; nevertheless, we can see the consequences of the Spirit's secret instrumentality in the miraculous experience of regeneration.

Regeneration is not a consequence of physical birth (it is "not of blood nor of the will of the flesh nor of the will of man, but of God," John 1:13). Neither is it a human achievement; on the contrary, it is the consequence of spiritual birth — it is "Not by might, nor by power, but by my Spirit, says the Lord of hosts" (Zechariah 4:6).

II

What were the consequences of the coming of God's Spirit on the day of Pentecost when ". . . suddenly a sound came from heaven like the rush of a mighty wind . . . . And they were all filled with the Holy Spirit. . . ."? The first consequence was that they ". . . began to speak in other tongues, as the Spirit gave them utterance" (Acts 2:2, 4).

At the Tower of Babel where men, in their pride and presumption, sought "to build a tower with its top in the heavens" (Genesis 11:4), God confused their language so that they were unable to understand one another's speech; on the day of Pentecost, God, through His Spirit, miraculously restored the gift of communication.

> Now there were dwelling in Jerusalem Jews, devout men from every nation under heaven. And at this sound the multitude came together, and they were bewildered, because each one heard them speaking in his own language. And they were amazed and wondered, saying, "Are not all these who are speaking Galileans? And how is it that we hear, each of us in his own native language? Parthians and Medes and Elamites and residents of Mesopotamia, Judea and Cappadocia, Pontus and Asia, Phrygia and Pamphylia, Egypt and the parts of Libya belonging to Cyrene, and visitors from Rome, both Jews and proselytes, Cretans and Arabians, we hear them telling in our own tongues the mighty works of God" (Acts 2:5-11).

" . . . God," the apostle affirms, "is not a God of confusion but of peace" (I Corinthians 14:33). With the descent of the Spirit on the day of Pentecost there was, among the babel of conflicting tongues, a renewal of meaningful communication.

At the beginning of creation, when the ". . . earth was without form and void, and darkness was upon the face of the deep. . ." (Genesis 1:2); the Spirit of God moved on the face of the waters, and the consequence was light in the midst of darkness and order instead of chaos. It is always so. When the Spirit of God descends there is an end to confusion and every evil work (cf. James 3:16-18).

III

Secondly, the consequence of the coming of the Spirit upon the apostles was the proclamation of the Gospel with saving power: there were added to the Church "about three thousand souls" (Acts 2:41).

What a contrast there is between the events associated with the giving of the law and those associated with the giving of the Spirit!

When Moses came down from the mount of God with the tables of the law in his hands he found the children of Israel practicing licentiousness and idolatry. In hot anger he broke the tables of the law on the ground, and, in the judgment which followed, "there fell of the people that day about three thousand men" (Exodus 32:28). When Peter, on the day of Pentecost, proclaimed the good news of the grace and the goodness of God, three thousand souls were added to the Church (Acts 2:41).

The law kills, the apostle reiterates, but the Spirit gives life (II Corinthians 3:6). On the day of Pentecost it was through the work of the Spirit of God that three thousand souls were brought into the fellowship of the Church.

IV

The third consequence of the Spirit's coming was a new sense of community: "And all who believed were together and had all things in common" (Acts 2:44).

Those who believed "devoted themselves to the apostles' teaching and fellowship, to the breaking of bread and the prayers" (Acts 2:42); but they soon came to the conclusion that those who share in spiritual things ought also to share in material things (cf. Romans 15:27): the consequence of this conviction was that all who believed "sold their possessions and goods and distributed them to all, as any had need" (Acts 2:44, 45).

The Jerusalem Christians sought to express the reality of their unity in the Spirit by a voluntary sharing of property and possessions. They understood that membership in the body of Christ implies a sense of genuine responsibility and concern for the needs of each member of the body. They spontaneously accepted what is today called the concept of mutual responsibility and interdependence. We ought, the apostle explains, to "bear one another's burdens, and so fulfill the law of Christ" (Galatians 6:2), for it is the duty of the strong to bear the burdens of the weak (Romans 15:1).

These converts to the faith took seriously the fact that "there is one body and one Spirit . . . One Lord, one faith, one baptism, one God and Father of us all" (Ephesians 4:4-6), and they were determined to express the reality of this subduing fact in the manner in which they shared their material possessions. They had grasped the apostolic truth that we are "one body in Christ, and individually members one of another" (Romans 12:5). For the early Christians this doctrine was not a pious platitude but a practical call to action. They voluntarily adopted the eminently sensible slogan: from each according to his ability, to each according to his need.

"God has made from one," the apostle states, "every nation of men to live on all the face of the earth" (Acts 16:26). Today this fact is all too often obscured by the perpetuation of national rivalries and ancient antipathies. Even within the Christian Church this fact of brotherhood finds tardy and inadequate expression. In the last analysis, it is God who makes men to be at unity in a house: that is why we need to pray that the wind of God's Spirit may enter our closed imaginations to sweep away the cobwebs of pride, prejudice, and partiality.

If we were really filled with the Spirit of God we would know what it means to be together and to have all things in common.

V

Finally, the consequence of the coming of the Spirit was joy: "And day by day, attending the temple together and breaking bread in their homes, they partook of food with glad and generous hearts, praising God. . . . " (Acts 2:46, 47).

Joy is a consequence of the coming of the Spirit of God. "The fruit of the Spirit," the apostle testifies, "is . . . joy" (Galatians 5:22).

" . . . do not get drunk with wine, for that is debauchery," the apostle admonishes, "but be filled with the Spirit. . . . " (Ephesians 5:18). Do not, he warns, get inebriated with wine (that leads to dissipation) but, on the contrary, get inebriated with the Spirit. The suggestion that there is a similarity between being drunk and being filled with the Spirit is startling and, at first sight, shocking, but it is also profoundly suggestive.

The fullness of wine and the fullness of the Spirit have this in common: that each is associated with an immediate feeling of exuberant well-being, of happy joy; the difference is that one is illusory and the other authentic, the one is an invitation to license and debauchery, the other to praise and gratitude. The apostle is careful to point out what are the concomitants of being filled with the Spirit. "Be filled with the Spirit," he enjoins; and then he adds, by way of explanation: "addressing one another in psalms and hymns and spiritual songs, singing and making melody to the Lord with all your heart, always and for everything giving thanks in the name of our Lord Jesus Christ to God the Father (Ephesians 5:19, 20).

William Tyndale, in the prologue to his English New Testament (1523) points out that Christianity, rightly understood, is

> Good, mery glad and joyfull tydings,
> that maketh a mannes hert glad,
> and maketh hymn singe,
> dance and leepe for joy.

Pascal speaks of the joy which accompanied what he called his "Divine Metamorphosis and miraculous transmutation."

For some time Pascal had developed, according to his sister, Jacqueline, an increasing "aversion for the follies and amusements of the world." On the night of November 23, 1654, he was meditating on the seventeenth chapter of St. John's Gospel when he had an overwhelming experience of the grace and goodness of God in forgiveness and acceptance. It was as though time stood still (he meticulously timed it, it lasted two hours) during which period of time he was conscious of nothing save the mystical presence of God. Immediately afterwards, Pascal wrote a detailed record of his experience on a piece of paper, an account of which he afterwards transcribed on a piece of parchment. Both copies were found after his death, carefully secreted and hidden in the lining of his coat.

The year of grace, 1654.
Monday, 23rd. November, Feast of S. Clement, Pope and
Martyr, and of others in the Martyrology
Vigil of S. Chrysogonus, Martyr, and others,
From about half-past ten in the evening until about
half-past twelve
FIRE
God of Abraham, God of Isaac, God of Jacob, not of the
philosophers and savants
Certitude. Certitude. Feeling. Joy. Peace.
God of Jesus Christ.
My God and Thy God
'Thy God shall be my God'
Forgetfulness of the world and of everything except God
He is to be found only in the ways taught in the Gospel
Grandeur of the human soul
Righteous Father, the world hath not known Thee, but I
have known Thee
Joy, joy, joy, tears of joy.

On the day of Pentecost there were those who misinterpreted the gift of tongues. These men, they mockingly accused, "are filled with new wine" (Acts 2:13). Peter promptly disabused them, pointing out the patent improbability of their explanation. " . . . these men are not drunk, as you suppose, since it is only the third hour of the day; but this is what was spoken by the prophet Joel: 'And in the last days it shall be, God declares, that I will pour out my Spirit upon all flesh' . . . " (Acts 2:15-17).

IV

"Technological civilization," C. Virgil Gheorghiu writes despairingly, "can create comforts but it cannot create the Spirit." Is this *The Twenty-Fifth Hour* when all hope is gone? [1]

To say this would be to reckon without the Spirit of God. That is why we may say, in a way, that Bob Dylan would not understand, that the answer is blowing in the wind.

---

[1] *Op. Cit.*, p. X.

Chapter Fourteen

BEGGARS BEFORE GOD

In a polished epigrammatic little poem, based upon the parable of the Pharisee and the tax collector, William Craw-shaw draws attention to the nature of the fundamental contrast:

> Two went to pray: oh! rather say,
> One went to brag: th' other to pray.
> One stands up close, and treads on high,
> Where th' other does not send his eye.
> One nearer to God's altar trod,
> The other to the altar's God. [1]

I

Lord Asquith, on a famous occasion, defined the Oxford manner as the effortless assumption of a conscious superiority. The Pharisees, in the time of Jesus, were tempted to make the same effortless assumption about their own superiority. They prided themselves on their religious zeal and on the manner in which they observed the detailed requirements of the religious law. They were scrupulous and meticulous: with intense carefulness they sought to keep themselves from ritual defilement and ceremonial uncleanness. And the consequence was a corrupting sense of moral superiority.

Tax collectors, by contrast, belonged to a class of men who were hated and despised. They were regarded by their countrymen as time-serving traitors, as quislings in the serv-

[1] *Divine Epigrams*

103

ice of the occupying power. There was nothing admirable about their occupation, and there was seldom anything admirable about their character. It was a man drawn from this group who provided the foil for the Pharisee that Jesus described.

Jesus, in this parable, paints an unforgettable picture with a few bold strokes. On the one hand, we have the portrait of a man who is inflated with a sense of his own impeccable righteousness and, on the other hand, the portrait of a man who is annihilated with a sense of his own unutterable shame. The one struts and preens himself in the very presence of God; the other abases himself in penitent sorrow.

II

"The Pharisee stood and prayed thus with himself . . ." (Luke 18:11). Standing was the usual posture for prayer, but there was something in the stance of this man that was symbolic and suggestive. There was somthing arrogant, something ostentatious, about the manner in which he took up his posture for prayer. He deliberately chose a prominent and conspicuous position, so that all men might see his piety, and observe his devotions.

Jesus records the subject matter of his prayer. It was not really a prayer at all; it was rather an exercise in self-congratulation. Jesus says he "prayed with himself": he addressed his prayer to God but in fact his prayer was directed not to God but to himself, to the extravagant praise of his own virtues.

"God, I thank thee that I am not like other men, extortioners, unjust, adulterers, or even like this tax collector. I fast twice a week, I give tithes of all that I get" (Luke 18:12, 13). He reminded God that he was superior to other men, not only in what he avoided but also in what he performed; not only in those vices from which he abstained — extortion and injustice and adultery — but also in relation to those pieties and charities which he performed. He was proud of his moral virtues and religious achievements, and he regarded these things as a proper ground for self-congratulation. He smugly compared himself with other men in general, and with this tax collector in particular. He eagerly used the tax collector as "a dark foil for his own gleaming whiteness." As he observed the tax collector standing afar off beating his breast with lowered head and downcast eyes, he thanked God that he did not need to beat his breast nor with shame to cast his eyes upon the ground.

Comparisons are always odious. Having made the flattering comparison, in the pleasing consciousness of his own rectitude, he proceeded to enumerate his accomplishments and achievements: "I fast twice a week, I give tithes of all that I get." It was far more than the law prescribed. Not only did he fast more than the law required — not once but twice a week — he also gave in excess of what was required — tithes of *all* his possessions. In the law tithes were only required of certain categories of goods — fruits of the field and the increase of cattle — but he tithed everything.

At first sight such impressive zeal might appear laudable. In actuality his real motive was to defeat the very purpose for which these divine ordinances were given. The institution of fasting was to remind men of their need for penitence and to inculcate a genuine sorrow for sin; the institution of tithing was to remind men of their indebtedness to God for all the gifts of life. This Pharisee, by exceeding the requirements of the law, was determined to make God his debtor: he was seeking to make the very institutions which remind us of our sin and need minister to his pride and self-conceit.

It is vitally important that we should understand the nature of his sin, lest we unwittingly share his guilt. This Pharisee was determined, by bestowing favors, to place God in his debt. He was eager to patronize God, to confer on Him a blessing and a favor, forgetting his own deep need for cleansing and forgiveness. Preoccupied with his own achievements and exalted by his own attainments, he was ignorant of the corruption of his own heart. God, so he inferred, was a lucky fellow to have such an excellent servant as himself.

Article Fourteen of the Thirty Nine Articles of Religion of the Church of England bluntly warns us against the sin which finds expression in the proud attempt to accumulate religious merit. We are debtors to God; that is why "Works of Supererogation" are not pleasing to God; when we have done all that is commanded we must say: "We are unworthy servants; we have only done what was our duty" (Luke 17: 10).

This Pharisee was blind to this truth. That is why his prayer contained no petition for forgiveness: he barricaded himself against the grace of God in the impregnable tower of his own self-righteousness.

By contrast, the tax collector stood "afar off" — he did not presume to enter into the Holy Place. He knew that his sins had set him at a distance from God and so he hesitated to draw near. In his bitter penitence he beat his breast, acknowledging that he deserved to be punished; in his shame he cast his eyes on the ground, overwhelmed by a sense of his own utter unworthiness. All he could say was: "God be merciful to me a sinner!" (Luke 18:13). There were no excuses, no comparisons, only the urgent cry, the passionate plea for mercy and forgiveness. The Pharisee placed himself in a class by himself: the highest class of the righteous; the tax collector likewise placed himself in a class by himself — but it was the lowest class of the sinful.

The tax collector had nothing of which to be proud; he had nothing to offer but his sin. He cast himself upon the mercy of God, and, because he sought mercy, he found mercy. The result is that he went down to his house "justified" — it is the technical Pauline word for acceptance with God. The Pharisee did not ask for mercy, and that is why he did not find it. It was there for him too, but he did not seek it.

The Pharisee spoke contemptuously of "*this* tax collector." Jesus took this term of contempt and turned it into a title of honor: ". . . *this* man went down to his house justified rather than the other; for everyone who exalts himself will be humbled, and he who humbles himself will be exalted"

(Luke 18:14). "God," the Apostle Peter solemnly warns, "opposes the proud, but gives grace to the humble" (I Peter 5:5).

III

It is always the humble who are blessed by God: those who acknowledge their spiritual poverty; those who confess, in the words of the dying Luther, that they are "beggars before God." That is what Jesus means when he says: "Blessed are the poor in spirit, for theirs is the kingdom of heaven" (Matthew 5:3). It is not the proud and the self-sufficient who inherit the kingdom of God, but those who, acknowledging their sinfulness and insufficiency, cast themselves on the mercy of God in Christ.

The parable of the Pharisee and the tax collector was spoken to those who trusted that they were righteous in themselves. It was not that they regarded themselves as righteous, but rather that they were possessed of a spirit of supreme self-confidence, that they had faith in themselves. The Apostle Paul reminds us that we must rely, "not on ourselves but on God. . ." (II Corinthians 1:9). The Apostle John puts it this way:

> If we say we have no sin, we deceive ourselves, and the truth is not in us. If we confess our sins, he is faithful and just, and will forgive our sins and cleanse us from all unrighteousness. If we say we have not sinned, we make him a liar, and his word is not in us (I John 1:8-10).

This salutary truth needs to be discovered by each self-sufficient man exalted by pride. "Oh the blessedness," writes Kierkegaard, "of knowing that we are always in the wrong as against God." The natural man knows nothing of this blessedness. In his arrogant pride he believes that he is not wrong, but right; he presumptuously imagines that he can justify himself, that he can put himself right with God by doing good works. The converted man gladly acknowledges his spiritual destitution. He freely confesses "that all [his] righteous deeds are like a polluted garment" (Isaiah 64:6). He does not therefore seek to establish his own righteousness; on the contrary, he seeks that righteousness which comes from God through faith (Romans 10:3).

IV

The really dreadful thing about pride is that it cuts a man off from God. "A proud man," C. S. Lewis rightly observes, "is always looking down on things and people: and, of course, as long as you're looking down, you can't see something that's above you." [2]

Pride not only blinds us to the truth about our relationship to God, it also blinds us to the truth about ourselves.

C. J. Dennis, the Australian poet, in a popular ballad, makes this point:

"Now come," said the Devil, he said to me,
   With his swart face all a-grin,
"This day, ere ever the clock strikes three,
   Shall you sin your darling sin.
For I've wagered a crown with Beelzebub,
Down there at the Gentlemen's Brimstone Club,
   I shall tempt you once, I shall tempt you twice,
   Yet thrice shall you fall ere I tempt you thrice."

"Begone, base Devil!" I made reply —
   "Begone with your fiendish grin!
How hope you to profit by such as I?
   For I have no darling sin.
But many there be, and I know them well,
All foul with sinning and ripe for Hell.
   And I name no names, but the whole world knows
   That I am never of such as those."

"How now?" said the Devil. "I'll spread my net,
   And I vow I'll gather you in!
By this and by that shall I win my bet,
   And you shall sin the sin!
Come, fill up a bumper of good red wine,
Your heart shall sing, and your eye shall shine,
   You shall know such joy as you never have known —
   For the salving of men was the good vine grown."

2 *Christian Behaviour* (London: Goeffrey Bles, 1943), p. 44.

"Begone, red Devil!" I made reply.
   "Parch shall these lips of mine,
And my tongue shall shrink, and my throat go dry,
   Ere ever I taste your wine!
But greet you shall, as I know full well,
A tipsy score of my friends in Hell.
     And I name no names, but the whole world wots
     Most of my fellows are drunken sots."

"Ah, ha!" said the Devil. "You scorn the wine!
   Thrice shall you sin, I say,
To win me a crown from a friend of mine,
   Ere three o' the clock this day.
Are you calling to mind some lady fair?
And is she a wife or a maiden rare?
     'Twere folly to shackle young love, hot Youth;
     And stolen kisses are sweet, forsooth!"

"Begone, foul Devil!" I made reply;
   "For never in all my life
Have I looked on a woman with lustful eye,
   Be she maid, or widow, or wife.
But my brothers! Alas! I am scandalized
By their evil passions so ill disguised.
     And I name no names, but my thanks I give
     That I loathe the lives my fellow-men live."

"Ho, ho!" roared the Devil in fiendish glee,
   " 'Tis a silver crown I win!
Thrice have you fallen! O Pharisee,
   You have sinned your darling sin!"
"But, nay," said I; "and I scorn your lure.
I have sinned no sin, and my heart is pure.
     Come, show me a sign of the sin you see!"
     But the Devil was gone . . . and the clock struck three. [3]

---

[3] *The Second Rhyme of Sym.*

Chapter Fifteen

THE FIRES OF GOD

Edith Sitwell, in an evocative poem pulsating with primitive and barbaric horror, pictures the time when, through the purging, purifying fires of God, men's hearts are cleansed.

> Gomorrah's fires have washed my blood —
> But the fires of God shall wash the mud
> Till the skin drums rolling
> The slum cries sprawling
> And crawling
> And calling
> "Burn thou me!"
> Though Death has taken
> And pig-like shaken
> Rooted and tossed
> The rags of me.
> Yet the time will come
> To the heart's dark slum
> When the rich man's gold and the rich man's wheat
> And the sea of the rich will give up its dead —
> And the last blood and fire from my side will be shed.
> For the fires of God go marching on. [1]

Freidrich von Logau, using a different metaphor, says the same thing:

> Though the mills of God grind slowly,
>   yet they grind exceeding small;
> Though with patience He stands waiting,
>   with exactness grinds He all. [2]

[1] *Gold Coast Customs.*
[2] *Sinngedichte,* III, ii, 24 (translated by H. W. Longfellow).

I

The theme of the parable of Dives and Lazarus is the certainty of retribution in relation to man's inhumanity to man.

There was a rich man, who was clothed in purple and fine linen and who feasted sumptuously every day. And at his gate lay a poor man named Lazarus, full of sores, who desired to be fed with what fell from the rich man's table; moreover the dogs came and licked his sores. The poor man died and was carried by the angels to Abraham's bosom. The rich man also died and was buried; and in Hades, being in torment, he lifted up his eyes, and saw Abraham far off and Lazarus in his bosom. And he called out, "Father Abraham, have mercy upon me, and send Lazarus to dip the end of his finger in water and cool my tongue; for I am in anguish in this flame." But Abraham said, "Son, remember that you in your lifetime received your good things, and Lazarus in like manner evil things; but now he is comforted here, and you are in anguish. And besides all this, between us and you a great chasm has been fixed, in order that those who would pass from here to you may not be able, and none may cross from there to us." And he said, "Then I beg you, father, to send him to my father's house, for I have five brothers, so that he may warn them, lest they also come into this place of torment." But Abraham said, "They have Moses and the prophets; let them hear them." And he said, "No, father Abraham; but if some one goes to them from the dead, they will repent." He said to him, "If they do not hear Moses and the prophets, neither will they be convinced if some one should rise from the dead" (Luke 16:19-31).

There are two characters and two scenes.

We think, in the first place, of the two characters: Dives and Lazarus. Lazarus is the only character in a parable to whom our Lord has given a personal name. Dives is not a proper name: it is simply the Latin word for "rich."

We are told that Dives was clothed in purple and fine linen. His clothing was costly and luxurious. Not only did he dress well; he lived well: he "feasted sumptuously every day." This suggests something of the gourmet, perhaps something of the glutton: every day he feasted sumptuously on expensive and exotic foods. The picture is one of ostentatious and selfish extravagance.

Lazarus, by contrast, was "full of sores," and "desired to be fed with what fell from the rich man's table." There were no table napkins: food was eaten with the fingers, which were dipped into the dish and cleaned on pieces of bread, which were then thrown away. It was these hunks of unwanted bread that Lazarus was eager to eat.

Lazarus was covered with ulcerated sores: "moreover the dogs came and licked his sores." The dogs of the East are not domestic pets; they are mangy snarling brutes. It was these scavenger dogs which came and licked his sores; and it was with these same scavenger dogs that he had to compete for bits of food.

As Dives is a picture of gross and extravagant self-indulgence, so Lazarus is a picture of abject misery and wretched poverty.

The contrast is absolute: on the one hand there is Dives, clothed with linen and fine clothes, on the other hand, Lazarus, covered with sores; on the one hand, Dives, who fared sumptuously every day, on the other hand, Lazarus, who hungered for the very crumbs that fell from the rich man's table; on the one hand, Dives, who had hired servants attending to his every need, on the other hand, Lazarus, whose only companions were the scavenger dogs of the street.

II

As there are two characters in the story, so there are two scenes.

The first is set in the context of this world; the second, in the next.

When Dives died he was buried, we may assume, with all proper pomp and purchased tears. No doubt there were hired mourners who accompanied his body to the grave and made loud lamentation; but, though his body was interred in a sepulchre of appropriate magnificence, his soul went to Hades.

Lazarus also died. We are not told that he was buried: perhaps his body was simply cast out into a pauper's grave for the vultures to devour but, in the other world, there was an escort of angels, waiting to carry him to Abraham's bosom.

The scene changes. Abraham, the father of the faithful, is presiding at a feast. Next to him, in the position of highest honor, is Lazarus, the one-time beggar. Dives speaks; he is in torment, and he begs for water.

Now there is a dramatic reversal of roles. Dives, who was so comfortable in this world, is now tormented. Lazarus, who was so miserable in this world, is now comforted.

Dives speaks: "Father Abraham, have mercy on me, and send Lazarus to dip the end of his finger in water, and cool my tongue, for I am in anguish in this flame." He thinks of Lazarus, the former beggar at the gate, and he begs Abraham to send Lazarus to perform this act of mercy. He still thinks of Lazarus as subservient to him.

Abraham reminds Dives that on earth he and Lazarus were separated from one another by a great gulf; they are still separated, but now the gulf is not temporal but eternal. "Son, remember that you in your lifetime received your good things, and Lazarus in like manner evil things; but now he is comforted here, and you are in anguish. And besides all this, between us and you a great chasm has been fixed, in order that those who would pass from here to you may not be able, and none may cross from there to us."

Dives apparently accepts his fate. He proceeds to intercede for the other members of the family: "Then I beg you, father, to send him to my father's house, for I have five brothers, so that he may warn them lest they also come into this place of torment." It suggests an attempt at self-justification. If only I had known, he seems to imply, I would not have come to this place of torment. Abraham replies immediately: "They have Moses and the prophets; let them hear them." Dives is urgent and insistent: "No, father Abraham; but if some one goes to them from the dead, they will repent." Abraham knows better: "If they do not hear Moses and the prophets," he repeats, "neither will they be convinced if some one should rise from the dead."

It was an accurate prognosis. A little later, a man with the name Lazarus was raised from the dead, having been dead four days. The immediate consequence of the raising of Lazarus was a determined plot, not only to destroy Jesus (John 11:47-53), but to put Lazarus to death (John 12:10, 11).

The fact is that men who are unmoved by the plain obligations of morality, men who are impervious to the appeal of charity and compassion, will be indifferent to the evidence of the supernatural. "If they can be inhuman with the Bible in their hands and Lazarus at their gates," James Denney affirms, "no revelation of the splendours of heaven or the anguish of hell will ever make them anything else." [1]

III

What was the sin of which Dives was guilty? He was, we are led to surmise, a respectable man. He had not issued axe handles to drive Lazarus from his gate; he had not been guilty of outrageous brutality.

He had done nothing in particular; and this is precisely the nature of his sin: he had done nothing. A rich man has a poor man at his gate, and he does nothing! Such callous indifference, such gross inhumanity, deserves, Jesus says, the damnation of hell.

We sin, not only by doing the things which we ought not to do, but also by failing to do the things which we ought to do. "Whoever knows what is right to do and fails to do it," James declares, "for him it is sin" (James 4:17).

Dives was condemned, not for what he did, but for what he failed to do; not for sins of commission, but for sins of omission.

IV

There are some who do not hesitate to say that America occupies a position in the world analogous to that of Dives in the parable.

[1] *The Way Everlasting* (London: Hodder and Stoughton, 1911), p. 171.

America is the richest nation in the world. To quote the President of the United States (in a speech at the National Convention of the Junior Chamber of Commerce), "Americans are the best fed, the best paid, and the best educated people in the world." The President went on to enumerate the measure of our wealth:

> We produce more goods; we transport more goods; we use more goods than anyone in the world.
>
> We own almost a third of the world's railroad tracks. We own almost two-thirds of the world's automobiles. We own half the trucks in the world. We own almost half of all of the radios in the world. We own a third of all of the electricity that is produced in the world. We own a fourth of all the steel. Although we have only about six per cent of the population of the world, we have half of its wealth.

"Bear in mind," the President continued, "that the other ninety four per cent of the world's population . . . would like to exchange places with us."

That is indeed the sober truth. At the gates of this fabulously rich nation are the nations of the Caribbean and Central and South America, and, further afield, the nations of Africa and Asia, and they desire to be fed with the crumbs that fall from the rich man's table. One third of the world goes to bed hungry every night: it is no wonder that multitudes are chronically debilitated and subject to endemic disease. In India the average daily wage, we do well to remember, is half a cent a day.

Lazarus lies at the gate full of sores; moreover the dogs of Communism are licking his sores.

The word that comes to us, as citizens as well as Christians, is "freely ye have received, freely give" (Matthew 10:8, KJV). "Every one," Jesus solemnly warns, "to whom much is given, of him will much be required" (Luke 12:48).

Are we guilty of the sin of indifference? Or have we a sense of deep responsibility for the impoverished people of the world? The Peace Corps, we may thankfully acknowledge, is perhaps indicative of a new spirit of positive and constructive concern.

On the day of judgment the simple and sufficient test by which all nations will be judged is the extent to which they have sought to serve Christ in the persons of those who suffer and are in need. To those on the right, the King will say:

"Truly, I say to you, as you did it to one of the least of these my brethren, you did it to me." But to those on the left, He will say: "Depart from me, you cursed, into the eternal fire prepared for the devil and his angels; for I was hungry and you gave me no food, I was thirsty and you gave me no drink, I was a stranger and you did not welcome me, naked and you did not clothe me, sick and in prison and you did not visit me" (Matthew 25:40-43).

Chapter Sixteen

DUNG AND SCUM

Some years ago, "Social Defaulters," in the Soviet Textbook of Law, were described, in emotive language, as "Mad dogs, rats, vermin, hyenas, dung and scum." The implications of this point of view are at once apparent: if social defaulters properly belong to the category of wild animals, then it is legitimate to destroy them, for we shoot mad dogs. Stalin acted on the logic of this assumption: during his reign of terror liquidation (to use the gruesome contemporary idiom) became an accepted instrument of government.

It is a depressing commentary upon the boasted progress of humanity that, in this century, millions of persons, in Germany and Russia, have been ruthlessly reduced on ideological grounds to dung and scum.

Richard L. Rubenstein draws attention to the sinister and suggestive fact that the Jews, in Hitler's Germany, were killed with an insecticide.

> Cyclon B was chosen because it could kill large numbers quickly and efficiently. It was a variant of Cyclon A, an *insecticide*. Cyclon was an abbreviation of the gas's most important ingredients, cyanide, choride, and nitrogen . . . . In Nazi propaganda the Jews were identified with lice, vermin, and insects, the very organisms for which an insecticide like Cyclon B was most appropriate.

These were also the organisms, he points out, "most intimately associated with the Devil, in mediaeval demonology.

117

These insects and detestable animals were also thought to be
the brood of fecal dirt and to find their nourishment and
habitat by wallowing in the small fecal dirt from which they
were spawned." The basic purpose of the death camps, he
accuses, was to turn the Jews into feces. [1]

I

Arthur Koestler, in a painful autobiographical fragment,
entitled, *Scum of the Earth,* describes his experiences in a
French concentration camp. He gives details of the manner
in which the inmates were systematically degraded and sa-
distically abused. He describes the daily mounting toll of
suffering and death. The camp cemetary, he bitterly observes, probably contains the most cosmopolitan collection
of skulls since the mass graves of the Crusades. Those who
survive, he opines, "wear the old school tie in the shape of
some scar on the body, or an ulcer in the stomach, or at least
a solid anxiety neurosis." [2]

Koestler believes that we urgently need to cultivate the
graces of tolerance and understanding. We need to discover
again what it means to be a man. We need to develop sympathy in the place of fanaticism; above all, we need "to
teach this planet to laugh again. At the moment we are still
howling like dogs in the dark."

Peter the Great, the ominous precursor of modern megalo-
maniacs, subscribed to the view that human beings are
cheap and expendable. On one occasion he was reproached
for the manner in which he had sacrificed the lives of his
people to construct St. Petersburg (a city which he intended
should perpetuate his name and which, by a strange irony of
fate, is now Leningrad). He laconically replied: "We must
break eggs to make omelet." The question we must ask is
this: Is man simply an egg to be broken (whether a "good
egg" or a "bad egg")?

Peter the Great, for his part, had no compunction about

[1] *After Auschwitz* (Indiana: Bobbs-Merrill, 1966), pp. 33-4.
[2] (New York: The Macmillan Company, 1941).

using men as manure with which to fertilize the ground for the future, as eggs to make omelet.

II

Today, we are beginning to realize that the sovereignty of God is the only adequate safeguard for the sanctity of man. "Where there is no God," Nicolas Berdyaev sagely comments, "there is no man either." "If God does not exist," proclaims Ivan Karamazov, "then all is permitted."

Nietzsche asks the rhetorical question "What thinker still needs the hypothesis of God?" "God," he insists, "is dead." The consequences of the death of God, he rightly foresees, will be dereliction and despair. When churches become the mausoleums of God, he proclaims, "then all the earth will writhe in convulsions. It will be the coming of nihilism." [3]

"The consequences of an attempt to find the whole meaning of man's life within the temporal," writes J. H. Oldham, "are becoming increasingly evident. If man is not made in the image of God, he has to be made in the image of society. He becomes a function of society, the instrument of impersonal ends. In the end he ceases to be a man. Life loses its sacredness. Where the interests of the state seem to require it, the individual may be ruthlessly sacrificed." [4] "A low and unspiritual view of man," Nathaniel Micklem warns, "is the prelude to inevitable slavery." [5]

Apart from the sovereignty of God man has no protection against the threat of progressive dehumanization. It is ominously significant that in 1944 it was necessary to add a new word to the vocabulary of the world: the sinister word genocide. Hitler decreed the final solution of the Jewish problem in the concentration camps of Belsen and Ausch-

---

[3] *The Complete Works of Frederick Nietzsche* (edited by Oscar Levy) (London: T. N. Foulis, 1911), VII, p. 43.

[4] *The Church and the Disorder of Society* (London: S. C. M., 1948), p. 140.

[5] *The Theology of Politics* (New York: Oxford University Press, N.D.), p. 26.

witz, of Buchenwald and Dachau. To serve the goal of Aryan purity six million persons in circumstances of unmitigated horror were systematically reduced to dung and scum.

III

Adolf Deissmann, in his celebrated book, *Light from the Ancient East,* quotes a letter from an Egyptian laborer to his wife who is expecting a baby. Deissmann summarizes the situation as follows:

> Hilarion is working for wages in the metropolis, Alexandria, and intends to remain there although his fellow-workmen are already about to return home. Anxiety is felt for him at home at Oxyrhynchus by his wife Alis, who is living with (her mother) Berus and (her only child) Apollonarin. She is expecting her confinement; gloomy thoughts arise within her: Hilarion has forgotten me, he sends neither letter nor money, and where is bread to come from for the growing family? She confides her trouble to her friend Aphrodisias, who is going to Alexandria, and through her Hilarion hears of his wife's sad case. He sends the letter: words merely, no money (the wages are said to be not yet paid), and in spite of tender lines for the child, in spite of the sentimental "How can I e'er forget thee?" nothing but brutal advice in the main: if it is a girl that you are bringing in the world, expose it.

Deissmann points out that there is a striking parallel in the *Metamorphoses* of Apuleius: a man setting out on a journey orders his wife, who is in expectation of becoming a mother, to kill the child immediately if it should prove to be a girl. [6]

In the ancient world infanticide was taken as a matter of course and was the most common form of family limitation. Unwanted children (particularly females) were "exposed": that is, they were left in desolate places, either to perish of exposure or to be devoured of beasts. Occasionally they were rescued by the owner of brothels for future employ-

[6] (Grand Rapids: Baker, 1965), pp. 169-70. Quoted by permission.

ment. Within a century and a half of Hilarion's letter to Alis the writer of the letter to Diognetus was able to boast that Christians do not expose their children.

In a world in which human life was cheap, Christians were responsible for bringing to birth a new respect for life. In the year 374 infanticide was made a crime.

After the conversion of the Emperor Constantine legislation was passed forbidding the branding of criminals and debtors on the face since man's face is the image of the divine beauty, and we ought not to deface the handiwork of God. Crucifixion, as a form of execution, and the breaking of the legs of criminals, was also abolished.

IV

In the year 1554 the Protestant scholar Muretus was carried to a hospital, desperately ill. He heard the doctors, who were ignorant of his identity, discussing in Latin the possibility of using him for a dangerous operation they were anxious to perform. One of the surgeons said, "Let the experiment be tried on this vile body." Came a voice from the bed, speaking in Latin: "Dost thou call that vile for which Christ was content to die?"

The rebuke was timely and it was just. Muretus did not say: "I am a scholar; I know Latin"; on the contrary, he knew that, in the last analysis, what gives human life its ultimate worth is the fact that Christ died for us. That is all, but that is enough.

This fact has profound implications. If we believe that Christ is the Saviour of all men (I Timothy 4:10) we dare not call any man common or unclean (Acts 10:28), for all men are the objects of His redemptive concern.

William Wilberforce believed that God had called him to labor for the abolition of the slave trade. He dedicated his time and his talents to the accomplishment of this task. He was ably supported by men of a like evangelical faith. Among this number was Josiah Wedgwood, famous for his pottery work. He designed a cameo showing, against a white background, a Negro kneeling in an attitude of piteous supplication, asking this question: "Am not I also a man and a brother?"

John Wesley was another who never ceased to thunder against what he called this "execrable sum of all villanies — traffic in African flesh." "I would to God that it might never be found more! That we might never more steal and sell *our brethren* like beasts," he said.

Six days before his death, Wesley addressed a letter of earnest encouragement to Wilberforce.

> Unless the Divine Power has raised you up to be as Athanasius, *contra mundum,* I see not how you can go through your glorious enterprise in opposing that execrable villainy which is the scandal of religion, of England, and of human nature. Unless God has raised you up for this very thing, you will be worn out by the opposition of men and devils; but *if God be for you, who can be against you?* Are all of them together stronger than God? Oh, *be not weary in well doing.* Go on, in the name of God and in the power of His might, till even American slavery, the vilest that ever saw the sun, shall vanish away before it.
>
> Reading this morning a tract wrote by a poor African, I was particularly struck by that circumstance that a man who has a black skin, being wronged or outraged by a white man, can have no redress; it being a *law* in our colonies that the oath of a black against a white goes for nothing. What villainy is this!
>
> That He who has guided you from your youth up, may continue to strengthen you in this and in all things, is the prayer of,
>
> Dear Sir,
Your affectionate servant,
John Wesley.

For Wesley, as for Wilberforce and Wedgwood, slavery was an offense both to God and man: a blasphemous con-

---

[7] Quoted, J. Wesley Bready, *England: Before and After Wesley* (London: Hodder and Stoughton, N.D.), pp. 228-9. Quoted by permission.

tradiction of God's purposes in creation and redemption and a denial of human brotherhood.

V

A Christian dare not say, with a contemptuous sneer, of any man, dung and scum; on the contrary, what he must say, with loving compassion, is: "the brother for whom Christ died" (I Corinthians 8:11).

Chapter Seventeen

ONCE TO EVERY MAN AND NATION

F. W. Robertson was a preacher of profound and penetrating insight. He had an intuitive understanding of the problems and preoccupations of men and women from every walk of life. He was, in the judgment of the poet Wordsworth, the outstanding religious teacher of the age. "He awakened," the inscription on his tombstone reads, "the holiest feelings in poor and in rich, in ignorant and learned."

Hensley Henson pays this tribute:

> He started with no special advantages of birth or wealth: he gained none of those academic distinctions which sometimes take their place: he won the patronage of no great man: and secured the public interest by no great book: he received no preferment: he formed no party: he never preached to the University either in Oxford, or in Cambridge: he was never invited to occupy the pulpit of Westminster or S. Paul's: he never preached at Court: no bishop complimented him with a chaplaincy: the only honorific position he ever held was that of High Sheriff's chaplain: he was the recipient of no honorary degree. Even the innuendoes and criticisms which he felt so deeply, and which his friends resented so bitterly, do not seem to have attracted much attention outside the little canting world of Brighton gossip. You may search the clerical biographies of the period in vain for any reference to his name.

[1] Quoted, Charles Smyth, *The Art of Preaching* (London: S.P.C.K., 1940), p. 225.

Add to this the fact that he died at the age of thirty seven, having published no book and printed no sermon; and that his posthumous fame rests on the shorthand notes made by a member of his congregation. And yet, in spite of this, he stands (in the opinion of Charles Smyth), in the front rank of English preachers "as the first and the greatest of the psychological preachers" of the nineteenth century.

I

One of his most famous sermons, preached on December 1, 1850, is entitled, "Three Times in a Nation's History," and it is based on the following passage of Scripture:

> And when he drew near and saw the city he wept over it, saying, "Would that even today you knew the things that make for peace! But now they are hid from your eyes. For the days shall come upon you, when your enemies will cast up a bank about you and surround you, and hem you in on every side, and dash you to the ground, you and your children within you, and they will not leave one stone upon another in you; because you did not know the time of your visitation" (Luke 19:41-44).

"These words," F. W. Robertson says, "which rang the funeral knell of Jerusalem, tell out in our ears this day a solemn lesson; they tell us that in the history of nations, and also, it may be, in the personal history of individuals, there are Three Times — a time of grace, a time of blindness, and a time of judgment . . . . When the Redeemer spake," he continues, "it was for Jerusalem the time of blindness; the time of grace was past; that of judgment was to come." [2]

II

There are three times, he notes, in a nation's history: first, a time of grace.

By the time of grace is meant the day of opportunity. For Jerusalem it was preeminently the time of our Lord's public ministry. But the city of Jerusalem was unresponsive to the message of the kingdom as preached by Jesus. Those who

2 *Sermons,* Fourth Series (London: Smith, Elder, 1866), p. 329.

saw the miracles which He performed did not see in these
works the indubitable hand of God; Jerusalem rejected both
the message and the ministry of Jesus, and therefore the
things that make for peace.

Jerusalem's day of opportunity, her time of grace, was
short: a brief three and a half years, the time of our Lord's
public ministry.

It is often so. A few brief actions may decide and determine the destiny of a nation or of an individual.

Sometimes God speaks but once. If not heard then, His
voice is heard no more. It is a perilous and fearful thing to
trifle with God's visitation in the day of grace.

For Jerusalem, the rejection and the crucifixion of Jesus
was followed by a time of blindness. The darkness that
enveloped the earth at the time of the crucifixion, blotting
out the sun (Matthew 27:45), was symbolic of a deeper
darkness that now enveloped Jerusalem. The day of opportunity was over and the day of judgment was about to begin.

It is a solemn fact of spiritual experience that there is
such a thing as moral blindness: a blindness which is an expression of God's judicial anger so that a man loses the
capacity to see.

The spiritual law is this: if a man will not see the truth,
if he deliberately shuts his eyes to the truth, then the result
is that he *shall* not see: God confirms the sentence and
withdraws the capacity to understand what is the truth. If
a man will not do the right when he knows the right, then
right becomes to him wrong, and wrong seems to him to be
right.

The time of blindness was but the prelude to the time
of judgment.

After Jesus spoke those words of tragic lament there was
an apparent calm, but it was only the strange and unnatural
stillness before the storm, in which every breath seems to be
hushed, and which is but the prelude to the moment when
the sky is lighted up with lightning flashes, and the whole
creation seems to reel.

Jerusalem was unaware that judgment was about to fall: when the battering rams of the Roman armies were hammering at the Tower of Antonia, the Jewish priests were still, in fancied security, celebrating their daily sacrifices.

There is a striking modern parallel. When the streets of Moscow were running with blood at the time of the Bolshevik Revolution, after the assassination of the Tsar and the murder of Rasputin, the priests of the Russian Orthodox Church, assembled in Holy Synod, were debating about the number of candles with which to adorn the altar.

It is perilously easy, Jesus warned, in picturesque phrase, to strain at a gnat and to swallow a camel (Matthew 23:24): to become preoccupied with the minutiae of religion and to neglect the weightier matters of the law — judgment, mercy, and truth. The Russian Orthodox Church was destined to recapitulate, in tears and torments, the tragedy of the Jewish Church at the time of the Fall of Jerusalem.

The siege of Jerusalem by the armies of Titus is one of the darkest in the pages of history. The Jewish historian, Josephus, says: "No other city ever suffered such miseries. It appears that the misfortunes of all men from the beginning of the world, if compared to those of the Jews, are not so considerable. The multitudes who perished exceeded all the destructions that man or God ever brought on the world"; within the city cannibalism was resorted to by the besieged survivors. Over 130,000 inhabitants finally perished, and 75,000 were sold into slavery.

III

We learn, from Jesus's heartbroken lament over the city of Jerusalem, that there are three times in a nation's history: a time of grace, a time of blindness, and a time of judgment.

Are we aware that this is, for the institutional church, a time of grace, unless (which God forbid!) it is already a time of blindness?

Are we aware that in Africa and Asia, as already in Russia and China, doors of opportunity for the preaching of the Gospel are being violently closed? And are we, as a consequence, determined to buy up the opportunities which remain? Bishop Stephen Neill, in his magisterial work, *Christian Missions*, sadly reports that, in the younger churches, there is far too much complacency, a lack of strategic vision, and little interest in evangelism.

And nearer home, the situation is no better. Confronted with revolutionary challenges of a changing social order, the institutional church projects, by and large, an image of reactionary stagnation. The horizons of the church are all too often petty and parochial: there is little attempt to play a role which is excitingly creative and fruitfully imaginative in relation to the problems of society. Too often the chuch reflects rather than reforms the life of society; too often the church is content passively to follow rather than courageously to challenge. Far from projecting an image of self-sacrificing activity, the church, all too often, projects an image of entrenched privilege and smug indifference.

God forbid that, in this time of grace, we should neglect the things that make for peace: the opportunity to establish brotherhood through the achievement of racial justice, the call to eliminate hardcore poverty through education and the creation of job opportunities, the challenge to abolish the scourge of war through international mediation and effective control, above all — the command to evangelize.

If we fail in this time of grace, this day of opportunity and challenge, it will not avail us to say that we have Calvin or Luther or Cranmer as our father, for God is able of these stones to raise up children to Calvin and to Luther and to Cranmer (*cf.* Matthew 3:9).

IV

Atheism, in this post-renaissance age (in the sober judgment of Alan Richardson) "has arisen chiefly as a revolt against the identification of Christianity with some outmoded system of thought or social order which is passionately felt to impede the progress of mankind in the direction of those very ideals which the Christian world view has itself made possible. It is a sobering thought for Christians that all the major atheistic movements of modern times, from the rationalism of the Enlightenment to the persecuting zeal of Marxist-Leninist materialism, are the bitter fruit of the Church's compromise with effete and repressive social systems or of her reluctance to embrace new ways of thought."

"We may notice," he adds reflectively, "how often a reasonable and humane person has become an atheist by way of reaction from stern conventionalism or saccharine sentimentality or intellectual laziness. . . ." [3]

Karl Marx was led to conclude that religion is the opium of the people. Charles Kingsley also came to the same conclusion. Religion, he accused, has been used as "an opium-dose for keeping beasts of burden patient while they are being overloaded." Communism, which is now supreme in vast areas of the world, is a judgment of God upon a degenerate church. "Those who cannot remember the past," George Santayana soberly observes, "are condemned to repeat it."

If we reject the call of Christ that comes to us in this time of grace, then we reject, says F. W. Robertson, our own salvation; and, in rejecting that, we bring on, in rapid steps, the day of judgment and of ruin.

[3] *Religion in Contemporary Debate* (Philadelphia: Westminster, 1966), p. 62. Quoted by permission.

Chapter Eighteen

THE PRESSURE TO CONFORM

Vance Packard's best seller, *The Hidden Persuaders*, is an account of the way in which "ad men" have become increasingly "depth men." He cites the testimony of Dr. Dichter, who contends that to sell a product it must appeal to feelings "deep in the psychological recesses of the mind." The important thing, he suggests, is to discover the psychological boost.

I

J. V. Langmead Casserley, in a brilliant caricature, illustrates the nature of our vulnerability. We are all, in our guilt and fear, snobbery and pride, he points out, easy game for those who would exploit us for their profit.

> I invent and patent, let us say, a new process for making socks out of seaweed. I persuade a considerable number of investors to join with me in equipping a large factory somewhere near the coast where plentiful supplies of seaweed can easily be obtained. I employ a considerable number of people to gather and process the seaweed. Thus a great deal of capital and labour is now bound up with this somewhat speculative and precarious enterprise. Only one difficulty remains. The public is on the whole quite satisfied with the socks it is wearing at present, and sees no particular reason for transferring its patronage to the new socks made out of seaweed. The plain fact is that the people left to themselves do not desire seaweed socks. And so I employ advertising experts, probably at fabulous expense, to set about the task of making people desire seaweed socks. There

are, of course, many stereotyped and well-worn ways of doing this. There is the sex angle: a beautiful young woman gazing with adoration at the handsome, perfectly tailored man, murmering as she does so, "Darling, there is a wild tang of the sea about you which sets my blood on fire." There is the Hollywood angle: "All the leading film actors are now wearing the new seaweed socks." There is the snob angle (for which a British setting may be preferred): the Lord Chancellor in his robes stands on the steps of the House of Lords, talking to the Archbishop of Canterbury, also in his robes; "Did you observe," His Lordship remarks to His Grace, "that all the dukes in the House this afternoon were wearing the new seaweed socks?" There is the fear-of-disease angle: "Do you realize that the man who wears the new seaweed socks is absorbing iodine into his system throughout the whole day?" There is the science angle: a young man in white overalls peers critically at an unidentified something or other in a test tube; "Seaweed socks are scientific socks!" And so it goes on. The diligent student of modern advertisements will no doubt imagine many more ways of inducing the public to desire these quite undesirable garments. Of course, all that the advertisements say about seaweed socks will be nonsense, and nine-tenths of it will consist of downright lies. Even the claims that have some vestige of truth in them will be exaggerated to a fantastic degree.

He soberly concludes: "The seaweed socks are, of course, an imaginary product; they are not more fantastic and ridiculous than a great many products which are in fact now on our markets and are widely advertised." [1]

II

We are all susceptible to the pressures of our peer group; we are all sensitive to sales talk; we are all vulnerable to manipulation and control.

It is mass production which, in the judgment of Dean Inge, has led to mass thinking. Modern man has become mass

[1] *The Bent World* (New York: Oxford University Press, 1955), pp. 117-8. Quoted by permission.

man. Aldous Huxley's *Brave New World* and George Orwell's *1984* are no longer mordant satires of tomorrow; they are lurid blueprints of today.

J. S. Whale analyzes the situation in which we find ourselves: "Personal idiosyncracies of opinion, thought or belief, are steadily being ironed out, as mass suggestion — ceaselessly conveyed through radio, television, cinema, press headlines, and the vast apparatus of high pressure advertisement — does its menacing work of standardization." The consequence of this remorseless process is that "the human person loses his distinctive, individual significance." He gloomily comments: "This darkness which covereth the earth is, over a vast area, gross darkness. Totalitarian systems leave no room at all for the dissident individual." [2]

In this twentieth century we have discovered, to our cost, that dissent and deviation spell death.

III

A corollary to this tendency to conformity, to standardization, is the belief that every man's opinion is as good as another's (an absurd view which no one accepts when it comes to traveling in an airplane or undergoing surgery), and the further assumption that, what everyone else does, we may do.

It is worth examining this point of view in relation to sexual morality.

Dr. Kinsey, who exhaustively investigated the sexual behavior of the human male and the human female, was largely responsible for the acceptance of views which, in relation to sexual morality, are basically behavioristic. Speaking of premarital intercourse, he writes:

> The fact that the single male, from adolescence to 30 years of age, does have a frequency of nearly 3.0 per week, is evidence of the ineffectiveness of social restrictions and the imperativeness of the biologic demands. For those who like

2 *The Protestant Tradition* (New York: Cambridge University Press, 1955), p. 230. Quoted by permission.

the term, it is clear that there is a sexual drive which cannot be set aside for any large portion of the population, by any sort of social convention. [3]

The late Dr. Kinsey was a professional zoologist: he applied the statistical methods which he successfully used in the study of gall wasps to the study of the human male and female. However, he was unable to see that sexuality in man is different from sexuality in animals. There is a fundamental difference between what a man can· do and what he *ought* to do, and this he was unable to perceive.

No one can read the reports without noting Dr. Kinsey's references to what he terms "normal" sexual behavior. We ought to regard sex, he says, as "a normal biologic function, acceptable in whatever form it is manifested." Is "normal" behavior, we may ask, the statistical average, or is it that which is in harmony with the true nature of man as a self-determining and morally responsible human being? Over and over again Dr. Kinsey makes disparaging judgments about traditional morality: he equates what is "average" with what is "normal," implying that what is "normal" is "right." It is the "biologic," he says, which should determine moral conduct and behavior. "By English and American standards," he concedes, "such an attitude is considered primitive, materialistic or animalistic, and beneath the dignity of a civilized and educated people." [4]

Millicent McIntosh, in a symposium that seeks to analyze and evaluate the findings of Dr. Kinsey, says that "the Kinsey Report uses all the techniques to which Americans are especially vulnerable. Its pages and pages of statistics, while dull and very depressing, are equally impressive to the ordinary person." A person's defenses can easily be broken down by the mere parade of these statistics, and their cunning exploitation.

[3] Alfred C. Kinsey, Wardell B. Pomeroy and Clyde E. Martin, *Sexual Behavior in the Human Male* (Philadephia: W. B. Saunders, 1948), p. 269. Quoted by permission.

[4] *Op. cit.,* p. 263.

> All boys and girls are pathetically anxious to be "normal."
> . . . They are especially vulnerable in the whole area of
> boy-girl relationships. Whatever is done by the crowd is
> what they must do, lest they risk being peculiar, blue stock-
> ing, prudish, with the inevitable result of unpopularity. So
> if the Kinsey Report announces that ninety-one per cent of
> females have done petting by the age of twenty-five, and
> eighty one per cent by the age of eighteen, the girl who is
> being pressed by a boy to go further than she thinks proper
> feels herself trapped by these statistics. If she is not erotic-
> ally aroused, or does not wish to be, she begins to wonder
> if she is normal. [5]

The difficulty arises from the acceptance of the unspoken but
implied assumption that what everyone does we may do, and
indeed ought to do.

IV

What the church needs and what the community needs
is men and women of courage and conviction who are willing
to court unpopularity by being different. "Any dead dog,"
it has been said, "can float downstream; it is only a live dog
that can swim against the current." Confronted by the
enormous pressures of a mass society, it is only men and
women of firm faith who can withstand in the evil day, and
having done all, to stand (Ephesians 6:13). Thus it was
that Shadrach, Meshach, and Abednego, being threatened
with living incineration in a fiery furnace, made the immortal
reply:

> If it be so, our God whom we serve is able to deliver us
> from the burning fiery furnace; and he will deliver us out
> of your hand, O king. But if not, be it known to you, O
> king, that we will not serve your gods or worship the golden
> image which you have set up (Daniel 3:17, 18).

Thus it was that Luther defied, in the name of truth, the
assembled might of the Holy Roman Empire at the Diet of
Worms, with the ringing declaration: "Here stand I; I can
do no other; so help me, God."

[5] D. P. Geddes (editor), *An Analysis of the Kinsey Reports on Sexual
Behaviour in the Human Male and Female* (New York: New American
Library of World Literature, 1954), Mentor edition, pp. 139-140.

V

C. A. Alington, late Head Master of Eton, using the eleventh chapter of the Epistle to the Hebrews as a model, has composed a modern version of the "Heroes of Faith."

By faith William Wilberforce removed from England the guilt of the African slave trade. By faith he, together with Thomas Clarkson, prepared the way for the abolition of slavery throughout the British Empire.

By faith Lord Shaftesbury gave up a life of peace and comfort to fight against apathy, prejudice, vested interests, and official obstruction, that hapless folks should receive compassion and that mercy should prevail in the land; by faith he forced through Parliament the first Factory Act forbidding the employment of children under nine in factories; by faith he made illegal the employment of women and little children in coal pits; by faith he brought to an end the barbarous practice of sending boys and girls of four and five years of age up the inside of chimneys to sweep them.

By faith David Livingstone set sail for Africa, and sojourned in that strange country, not knowing whither he went; by faith he penetrated to the heart of the dark continent, bringing to light hidden iniquities and age-long cruelties; by faith he opened the way to the coming of the Gospel with healing and freedom in its wings.

By faith Florence Nightingale, when she was come to years, refused to be called the daughter of her wealthy father, choosing rather to suffer affliction in service to the neglected children to God than to enjoy the pleasures of London in the Season; by faith she led a band of trained nurses to care for the untended sick and wounded in the Crimea; by faith she overcame the obstacles of Army and Medical etiquette; by faith she passed through the Sea of Red Tape as by dry land, which the authorities essaying to hinder were put to confusion; by faith she created Sick-nursing as a ministry of enlightened skill, making science the handmaid of mercy.

These all died in faith, not having received the promises, but having seen them afar off, and embraced them, and confessed that they were but pioneers on the earth.

By faith William Booth and Catherine his wife endured ridicule, obloquy and violence to carry the Gospel to the slums of Darkest England; by faith they brought Christian compassion to rescue the poorest and most forlorn.

By faith the founders of the Church Missionary Society set forth to repair the manifold wrongs done to Africa; by faith their missionaries went to India, China and Japan, not fearing the wrath of kings or princes, for they endured as seeing Him Who is invisible; by faith they penetrated into Uganda and were not afraid of the king's commandment, so that in very truth there sprang of one, and him as good as dead, as many as the stars of the sky in multitude and as the sand that is by the sea-shore innumerable.

And what shall I more say? For time would fail me to tell of Richard Cobden and John Bright; of James Simpson and Lord Lister; of William Carey, Alexander Duff and John Howard; of Mary Slessor also, Josephine Butler, and Elizabeth Fry; of Captain Scott, and Lawrence Oates (who being dead yet speaketh); and of all who through faith removed mountains, drained marshes, laid submarine cables, irrigated desert land; who reformed prisons, and changed the hell of lunatic asylums into a haven of mercy; found alleviation for pain; taught the blind to read; gave ears to the deaf; brought hope to the leper; who won for all children the chance of education; redressed ancient wrongs; achieved long-cherished hopes; cured incurable diseases, so that women received their dead restored to life again; others endured cruel sufferings — mockings, slanders yea, moreover, bonds and imprisonment; some were killed while experimenting for the good of mankind, some lost fingers, arms, and life itself through working with deadly rays, dying that others might live; young men spent the best years of their lives in the trenches, amid rending steel and scorching flame and rats and lice and the stench of putrefying corpses; they were gassed; they were bayoneted; they were shot down from the sky on fire; they were drowned in the depths of the sea (of whom their world was not worthy); they campaigned in deserts and over mountains and dwelt in dens and caves of the earth.

Wherefore, seeing we also are compassed about with this great cloud of witnesses to the power of faith, let us lay

aside all that might hamper our running, and let us run
with unswerving purpose the course that is set before us,
looking unto Jesus, Who trod the path of faith before us
and trod it to the end. [6]

[6] A *Dean's Apology* (London: Faber and Faber, 1952), pp. 197-199.
Quoted by permission.

Chapter Nineteen

THE NOBLE ARMY OF MARTYRS

In the city of Prague there is a monument to the memory of John Hus, the revered Bohemian reformer. Hus's own clarion words are inscribed on the monument: "Let each man be free to confess the truth."

John Hus, however, was not permitted to confess the truth he had come to believe. He was, on the contrary, denied the rights of conscience and condemned to die.

I

Hus, a man of pure and austere life, had become increasingly concerned about the notorious immoralities of the clergy, and, at Synod convention in Bohemia, had fearlessly denounced the prevalent corruption of the church.

> Among the clergy a monstrous prodigy has arisen upon earth: high in rank, low in spirit; a proud office, an abased life; a busy tongue and a lazy hand; much talk and little fruit; a severe face and light conduct; vast respect, little constancy; a blind watcher, a dumb herald, a crippled warrior, a doctor ignorant of medicine; stupid, dirty tipplers, priestly vessels full of rotten morals which are an abomination to God. There are among you, prelates, canons, and priests, many who live with women whom they idolize, burning with lust and love. And you, unholy vessels of priests, who first have smirched yourselves with whores and still have adulterous thoughts, do you dare thus to take into you the sacrament which has all deliciousness and all sweet-

ness? Do you not fear that the wrath of God may smite you? There are many among you who besmirch themselves with intoxication and drunkenness far more scandalously than the laity; they go, stick in hand, to the ale house, like the laity to the threshhold of the saints, and when they return home they can hardly walk, still less speak, and least of all know what their priestly dignity demands. The richer among you visit each other for entertainment at the expense of the alms, and food and drink are richer and more abundant, costlier and more delicate, than among the wealthy citizens and noblemen. Not even while celebrating the Mass can they drop their unseemly, arrogant, immoral and greedy conversations. Verily, they, more than dogs, should be driven forth from services. [1]

His enemies succeeded in persuading the pope to issue a bull (1405) condemning the false teaching being propagated in Bohemia. In 1408 Synod prohibited public preaching against the immoralities of the clergy. Hus protested: "In matters of the soul God must be obeyed before man." Another papal bull was issued: Hus appealed from the "misinformed pope to the pope who might be better informed." Hus was excommunicated and summoned to Bologna. He was not afraid of martyrdom — he longed to embrace it — but he wondered whether the longing might not also be a seduction. He was suddenly aware of his life as a unique and precious gift which he would not and must not throw away: death was a great sacrifice, not to be made meaninglessly. This also was a radical departure from the tradition of the Middle Ages. He refused to go.

The last three years were years of intense creative activity. Up until that time he had preached in Czech but written in Latin. He now wrote in Czech, making the clumsy Czech language, saturated with foreign words, expressive and pliable. He made Czech a literary language. In fact, he did for the Czechs what Wycliffe did for the English and Luther

[1] Quoted, Paul Roubiczek and Joseph Kalmer, *Warrior of God: The Life and Death of John Hus* (London: Nicholsen and Watson, 1947), pp. 76-7.

for the German: he completed the translation of the Bible and made it accessible to the people.

Hus openly attacked the mercenary sale of indulgences. The combination of money with the forgiveness of sins was unequivocally mortal sin: it was simony. ". . . freely have ye received," Jesus said, "freely give" (Matthew 10:8, KJV). The true essence of repentance was completely falsified through indulgences. "By such indulgences the foolish rich are led to cherish vain hopes, the laws of God are held in contempt, the unschooled populace more readily become sinners, heavy sins are accounted but light, and the people in general are plundered."

Hus was summoned to Constance. The Emperor Sigismund urged Hus to appear before the Council to plead his own cause. The Emperor offered Hus his safe conduct. On his arrival in Constance the Pope also assured him of his safety and protection. Hus, stirred only by his desire for greater holiness in the Church, believed that he could move the Council as he had moved his own congregation. He wished only for an opportunity of setting forth his opinions before assembled Christendom, and thought that their manifest truth could not fail to carry conviction. Hus, however, was immediately arrested. It was impossible, his captors said, to break faith with one who had already broken faith with God.

The Council refused to hear Hus's defense. He was placed in close confinement and cruelly treated. He became dangerously ill and was in danger of death.

Hus's guilt was clear. His writings, it was said, contained opinions contrary to the systems of the Church; he had openly acted in defiance of ecclesiastical authority. Efforts were made to secure a retractation. "I stand," he boldly replied, "at the judgment seat of Christ, to whom I have appealed, knowing that He will judge every man, not according to false or erroneous witness, but according to the truth and each one's deserts." Hus thus asserted against authority the rights of the individual conscience, and removed his cause from the tribunal of men to the judgment seat of God.

The Council passed sentence:

> Under an appeal to the Name of Christ, the holy Synod of Constance decides, announces and declares, that John Hus has been and still is a proved and open heretic who has taught errors and heresies long denounced by the Church, and also much that is troublous, objectionable, audacious and seditious, preaching all this to the no small offence of the divine Majesty and the whole Church and to the damage of Catholic belief; that he has scorned the keys and censure of the Church and has persisted in such obduracy for many years, and thereby, with a contempt of the Church authorities, has in an insulting and annoying way appealed to the Lord Jesus Christ as the highest judge. In view of this the holy Synod declares John Hus to be a heretic and as such judged and condemned. It also decides because it recognizes him as a stubborn, incorrigible man who is not ready to abjure his false doctrines and heresies that he shall be deprived and degraded of all the priestly and other dignities with which he is invested. [2]

At the stake Hus said: "I am prepared to die in that truth of the Gospel which I taught and wrote."

John Hus died for the rights of conscience. At his trial he testified: "These bishops demand of me that I should recant and abjure, but I fear to do so lest I lie in the eyes of God and offend my conscience and God's truth."

He would recognize no other sovereignty than the sovereignty of truth. "From the earliest days of my studies," he steadfastly affirmed, "I have abided by this my rule that as soon as I learn to know sounder opinion, with joy and in all humility I abandon the earlier one." He therefore refused to retract real or supposed errors; he asked to be taught and convinced by arguments. "I am humbly ready," he confessed, "to retract anything that shall be proved erroneous to me according to the Scriptures."

[2] *Op. cit.*, p. 239.

Thus Hus, by his brave martyrdom, defended the rights of conscience and affirmed the sovereignty of truth.

II

Down the ages there have been many who, being threatened with fire and faggots, have replied: "Here stand I; I can do no other; so help me, God."

It was Luther who boldly said: "Unless I am convicted by Scripture and plain reason, my conscience is captive to the Word of God. I cannot, and I will not, recant anything, for to go against conscience is neither right nor safe."

Polycarp's name stands high in the role of the noble army of martyrs. He was Bishop of Smyrna when the fires of persecution reached Asia Minor in the year A.D. 155. He was brought before the magistrate and accused of being a Christian. The magistrate was greatly moved by his venerable age and was reluctant to condemn him. He pleaded with Polycarp to offer incense to the image of Caesar. "What harm is there," he asked, "to say Lord Caesar and to offer incense and all that sort of thing, and to save yourself?"

Polycarp was unmoved by such prudential considerations of self-preservation. He quietly replied: "I am not going to do what you advise me." He was led to the arena where again the proconsul urged him to deny the faith.

"Have respect for your age," he said. "Take the oath and I shall release you. Curse Christ."

Polycarp made the memorable reply: "Eighty six years I have served Him and He never did me any wrong. How can I blaspheme my King who saved me?" So they brought him to the stake where he prayed: "O Lord God Almighty, the Father of Thy well beloved and ever blessed Son . . . I thank Thee that Thou hast graciously thought me worthy of this day and this hour."

What are we to make of such inflexibility? Such courage? Such constancy? Are we to dismiss such resolute persistence as obsessional fanaticism? A painful and pathetic example of latent masochism?

Such facile explanations clothed in psychological jargon are singularly unconvincing. We dare not explain, and thereby explain away, a man's deepest convictions as a matter of glands and of genes. There is such a thing as truth which an honest man is bound to defend, and there is such a thing as conscience which a religious man is bound to obey.

In these days of latitudinarian accommodation, it may be difficult for those who confuse conviction with obstinacy and belief with opinion to sympathize with, let alone to understand, the faith of men whose one consuming passion was to serve Christ, whose one consuming desire was to please God.

III

Suffering is an inescapable concomitant of Christian discipleship. "If any man would come after me," Jesus warned, "let him deny himself and take up his cross and follow me" (Matthew 16:24). For many it has been a literal cross; the price of obedience has been death. It is not without significance that the word martyr and the word witness are etymologically the same, for a martyr *is* a witness unto death.

The noble army of martyrs have had their successors in every age. Bishop Hugh Latimer and Bishop Nicolas Ridley were notable martyrs of the English Reformation. They died in circumstances of harrowing brutality. The words of the older man to the younger, as the procession reached the funeral pyre, are worthy of perpetual remembrance: "Be of good comfort, Master Ridley, and play the man. We shall this day light such a candle, by God's grace, in England, as I trust shall never be put out."

Scholars have recently discovered, among the disbursements of the Oxford bailiffs, Winkle and Wells, the following items:

For three loads of wood faggots to burn Ridley and Latimer	12 shillings
Item, one load of fir faggots	3 shillings 4 pence
For the carriage of these four loads	2 shillings

Item, a post	1 shilling 4 pence
Item, two staples	6 pence
Item, four labourers	2 shillings 8 pence

This melancholy list makes poignant and painful reading.

A little later Archbishop Thomas Cranmer was burned at the same place. The memorial inscription reads:

To the glory of God and in grateful commemoration of Thomas Cranmer, Nicholas Ridley, Hugh Latimer, Prelates of the Church of England, who, near this spot, yielded their bodies to be burned, bearing witness to the sacred truth which they had affirmed and maintained against the errors of the Church of Rome, and rejoicing that to them it was given, not only to believe in Christ but also to suffer for His sake, this monument was erected.

The same price had been paid by those who, in this twentieth century, have been the helpless and hapless victims of totalitarian tyranny. The enemies of God use the weapons of terror and torture, even though it is the concentration camp and the gas oven rather than the arena and the lions. The methods may be new but the results are the same. Today, as always, men are urged to deny the truth by threats of brutal battery and bloody death, and still, in obedience to conscience and in loyalty to God, men and women seal their testimony with their blood. The toll is not yet complete: those whom they cannot persuade they seek to coerce, and those whom they cannot compel they seek to destroy.

The final word, however, is not with those that take the sword, for in the end they that take the sword will perish by the sword. The last word is not with man but with God. The powers of this world may make their inventory; they may list their wood and their nails, their staples and their chains, but, for the faithful who love not their lives unto death, there remains an eternal weight of glory. Their affliction is but for a moment, but their reward is forever.

IV

The path of obedience is often costly and it is always lonely. "Enter by the narrow gate," Jesus said, "for the gate is wide and the way is easy, that leads to destruction, and those who enter by it are many. For the gate is narrow and the way is hard, that leads to life, and those who find it are few" (Matthew 7:13, 14). Nevertheless, there is a reward. ". . . I saw the souls of those who had been beheaded for their testimony to Jesus and for the word of God, and who had not worshiped the beast or its image and had not received its mark on their foreheads or their hands," the Apostle John proclaims, "and they reigned with Christ" (Revelation 20:4).

Chapter Twenty

HOLD MY RIGHT HAND

D. S. Merezhkovsky, in a pioneer study, draws attention to the way in which, with consummate genius, Tolstoy uses, in *War and Peace,* physical characteristics to express character. [1] As Napoleon gives a Russian soldier the Legion of Honor, he "draws off the glove from his *white small hand.*" Nicolai Rostov remembers "that self-satisfied Bonaparte with his *little white hand.*" When Napoleon talks with the Russian diplomat, Balashiev, he makes "an energetic gesture of inquiry with his *little white, plump hand.*"

Later, Tolstoy fills out the picture. He describes the upstart Emperor in his tent before the battle of Borodino:

> Snorting and panting, he turned, now his plump back, now his overgrown fatty chest to the brush with which the valet was rubbing him down. Another valet, holding the mouth of the bottle with his finger, was sprinkling the pampered little body with eau-de-cologne, with an air that said he alone could know how much and where to sprinkle. Napoleon's short hair was damp and hanging over his forehead. But his face, though bloated and yellow, expressed physical well-being. "More now, harder now!" he cried, stretching and puffing, to the valet who was rubbing him, then bending and presenting his fat shoulders.

Speranski is another self-made demi-god, and he, too, has white fat hands. "Prince Andrei watched all Speranski's movements; but lately he was an insignificant seminarist,

[1] *Russian Literature and Modern English Fiction,* edited by Donald Davie (Chicago: The University of Chicago Press, 1965), p. 123 et seq. Quoted by permission.

and now in his hands, those white plump hands, he held the fate of Russia, as Volkonski reflected." "In no one had the Prince seen such delicate whiteness of the face, and still more the hands, which were rather large, but unusually plump, delicate and white. Such whiteness and delicacy of complexion he had only seen in soldiers who had been long in hospital." A little later he again "looks involuntarily at the white delicate hands of Speranski, as men look generally at the hands of people in power. The mirror-like glance and the delicate hand somehow irritated Prince Andrei."

Whereas Pushkin, Tolstoy remarked, was content to depict a physical characteristic lightly, and, as it were, incidentally, it was his practice, he explained, to set it forth distinctly. In all literature there is no writer equal to Tolstoy in depicting the human body. D. S. Merezhkovsky observes:

> At the first appearance of Old Prince Volkonski we get only a fleeting sketch, in four or five lines, "the short figure of the old man with the powdered wig, small *dry hands* and grey, overhanging brows that sometimes, when he was roused, dimmed the flash of the clever youthful eyes." When he sits down to the lathe "by the movement of his small foot, the firm pressure of his *thin veined hand* you could still see in the Prince the obstinate and long-enduring force of hale old age. . . "

> Or take the effect of Vronski when he first sees Anna Karenina. You could see at a glance she belonged to the well-born; that she was very beautiful, that she had red lips, flashing grey eyes, which looked dark from the thickness of the lashes, and that "an excess of life had so filled her being that in spite of herself it showed, now in the flash of her eyes, now in her smile." And again as the story progresses, gradually, imperceptibly, trait is added to trait, feature to feature: when she gives her hand to Vronski he is delighted "as by something exceptional with the vigorous clasp with which she boldly shook his own." When she is talking to her sister-in-law Dolly, Anna takes her hand in "her own vigorous little one." The wrist of this hand is "thin and tiny," we see the "slender tapering fingers," off which the rings slip easily.

In the hands of Karenina there is yet greater expressiveness than in the face. In the hands of Anna lies the whole charm of her person, the union of strength and delicacy. [2]

Tolstoy knew that the language of gesture, if less varied than words, is more direct and immediate. He therefore used external physical characteristics as a device by which to portray the secret inner life of his characters. And it may be, Merezhkovsky suggests, that Tolstoy paid much attention to the hands because they are the only part of the human body always bare and near elemental nature, and unconcious as the animal.

I

W. E. Sangster, in a graphic passage, points out that no other part of our body has so worked itself into common speech.

"To lend a hand" is a fine expression of service,
"To be a poor hand" is definite condemnation,
"To come cap in hand" is a sign of servility,
"To be an old hand" is a mark of ripe experience,
"To come with an empty hand" is a sign of poverty or meanness,
"To rule with a heavy hand" is to make him your first assistant,
"To get one's hand in" is to become familiar with the work,
"To take a thing in hand" is to make it a serious undertaking,
"To act with a high hand" is to be arrogant,
"To have clean hands" is to be incorruptible,
"To have one's hands full" is to be completely occupied,
"To be a handful" is to be nuisance,
"To wash one's hands of a thing" is to abandon it entirely,
"All hands on deck" is the cry of an hour of danger,
"Hands off" is a serious warning not to be ignored, and
"Hands up!" is the cry of the gangster.

Our five senses, he continues, are inferior to those of the lower creatures. We have not an eye as sharp as the eagle's, nor a nose as keen as a dog's. We have not an ear as alert

[2] *Op. cit.*, p. 129.

as the horse, nor a touch as sensitive as a spider's; but we outsoar all the lower creatures with our hands. [3]

The human hands are instruments of astonishing and amazing dexterity. With our hands, C. FitzSimons Allison pointedly reminds us, we count money, bend beer cans, write checks, make biscuits, become fists, point fingers, remove cancers, dig ditches, shoot guns, and deliver babies. [4]

Our hands are expressive of our deepest personality. With our hands we speak, without premeditation, spontaneously and naturally. That is why portrait painters of eminence like to paint, not only the faces, but also the hands, of their subjects.

II

Our hands speak of our capacity for good and evil.

It is with the same hands that we create the music of Bach and Beethoven that we defoliate the villages of Viet Nam, it is with the same hands that we help that we also hurt, with the same hands that we pray that we also slay.

Our hands speak eloquently of our moral dubeity. All things, however, are open and laid bare to the eyes of Him with whom we have to do (Hebrews 4:13); and God is not deceived. He knows the measure of our dissimulation and the nature of our guilt.

> When you spread forth your hands,
>   I will hide my eyes from you;
> even though you make many prayers,
>   I will not listen;
>   your hands are full of blood (Isaiah 1:15).

The Psalmist asks the rhetorical question:

> Who shall ascend the hill of the Lord?
> And who shall stand in his holy place?

And he replies:

> He who has clean hands and a pure heart
>   Who does not lift up his soul to what is false
>   and does not swear deceitfully (Psalm 24:4).

[3] *Westminster Sermons* (Tennessee: Abingdon Press, 1960), Volume I, p. 88. Quoted by permission.

[4] *Fear, Love and Worship* (New York: Seabury, 1962), p. 129.

The tragedy is that we neither have clean hands nor a pure heart. But that is not the full measure of our guilt. We have lifted up our hands, not only against man but against God. "Jesus of Nazareth," Peter accused, "ye have taken and by wicked hands have crucified and slain" (Acts 2:23, KJV). "We have killed him," Nietzsche proclaims. "How shall we, the murderers of all murderers, comfort ourselves? What was holiest and most powerful of all that the world has yet owned has bled to death under our knives. Who will wipe this blood off us? What water is there for us to clean ourselves?"

The Gospel is that even the blood of deicide can be washed away, because God has opened, through the blood of Jesus, a fountain to cleanse from sin and all uncleanness (Zechariah 13:1). The Gospel is that

he was wounded for our transgressions,
he was bruised for our iniquities;
upon him was the chastisement that made us whole,
and with his stripes we are healed (Isaiah 53:5).

The Apostle Peter says the same thing: "He himself bore our sins in his body on the tree... By his wounds," he points out, "you have been healed" (I Peter 2:24).

In the Lord's Supper we have a perennial reminder of this fact. "It is into the calloused empty instruments of our guilt and shame, our inadequacy and self sabotage" (to quote Allison's fine words) that the bread and the wine is placed. "When I take the service of Holy Communion," Sangster says, "I do not see faces; I only see hands. How I exult in their variety; all reaching out for the bread which is His body and the wine which is His blood; all making their mute demand for that which Jesus will not deny: the large hands of men; the small hands of women; the smooth hands of the clerk; the rough hands of the manual worker; the soft hands of the woman of leisure; the coarse hands of those who have found life hard; the shapely hands of the maiden and the shrivelled hands of the old — all different, and all equal at the Table of the Lord." [5]

[5] *Ibid*, p. 89. Quoted by permission.

But the service of Holy Communion speaks not only of our need but also of His forgiveness, not only of our guilt but also of His grace. We stretch our hands to Him and into our hands He places the broken bread of His body, given for us, and the cup of His blood, shed for us. "The cup of blessing which we bless, is it not a participation in the blood of Christ?" the apostle demands: "The bread which we break, is it not a participation in the body of Christ?" (I Corinthians 10:16).

There is a moment of moving pathos in Hemingway's Nobel Prize winning novel, *The Old Man and the Sea,* when the boy goes to visit the old man in his shack and he sees his lacerated hands. "He was asleep when the boy looked in the door in the morning. It was blowing so hard that the drifting boats would not be going out and the boy had slept late and then come to the old man's shack. . . The boy saw that the old man was breathing and then he saw the old man's hands and he started to cry. He went out very quietly . . . and all the way down the road he was crying." [6]

The hands of Jesus, with which He blessed little children, are the hands which we nailed to a tree. When we think of this, in the sacrament of Holy Communion, we are filled with penitence and shame.

III

The Christian man knows both what it is to be forgiven of God and also what it is to be upheld of God. "Thou dost hold my right hand," the Psalmist joyfully exclaims (Psalm 73:23).

A man's right hand is the hand with which he works: it is the instrument and symbol of his strength and skill. It is the right hand which we extend in greeting: when we go forth to meet another, we stretch out our hand; when we have established a relationship of confidence and trust, we confirm it by clasping hands.

We do not, however, extend the right hand of fellowship to God. It is God, as Karl Barth reminds us, who holds us

[6] (New York: Scribner's and Son, 1952), pp. 134-35.

by *our* right hand. It is God who takes the initiative in stretching forth His hand to save us (*cf.* Matthew 14:31). And it is God who, in soveriegn mercy, continues to uphold us with His sure word of promise. "I give them," Jesus says, "eternal life, and they shall never perish, and no one shall snatch them out of my hand" (John 10:28).

In this confidence we need not fear.

> I said to the man who stood at the Gate of the Year,
> "Give me a light that I may tread safely into the unknown,"
> And he replied: "Go out into the darkness, and put your
>   hand into the Hand of God.
> That shall be to you better than light, and safer than a
>   known way."
>
> So I went forth,
> And finding the Hand of God, trod gladly into the night.
> And He led me towards the hills and the breaking of day
>   in the lone East.
> So heart be still;
> What need our little life, our human life, to know, if God
>   hath comprehension?
> In all the busy strife, of things both high and low,
> God hideth His intention.
> God knows. His will is best.
> The stretch of years which wind ahead, so dim to our im-
>   perfect vision,
> Are clear to God. Our fears are premature; in Him all time
>   hath full provision. [7]

---

[7] M. L. Haskins.